GREATER

Richmond

REGION ON THE RISE

INTRODUCTION BY STEVE CLARK ★ ART DIRECTION BY BRIAN GROPPE

GREATER

Richmond

REGION ON THE RISE

★ SPONSORED BY THE GREATER RICHMOND CHAMBER OF COMMERCE

URBAN
TAPESTRY
SERIES
TOWERY
PUBLISHING, INC.

Contents

By Steve Clark

OME YEARS AGO—IN THE MID-1980S, IF MEMORY SERVES—RICHMOND WAS IN the market for a fresh slogan, one that would entice tourists to bring money to town and convince industries to relocate here.

No one asked for my two cents' worth. Nevertheless, I gave it a go. I donned my frayed thinking cap, planted my tongue firmly in cheek, and came up with a slogan I thought was perfectly suitable for Richmond, given all that has happened here during the city's long and storied history.

Borrowing the theme of a familiar spiritual hymn, I suggested: "Richmond: Nobody knows the trouble we've seen."

Understandably, my slogan did not stand a snowball's chance in Virginia on the Fourth of July of ever being printed on a tourism brochure or bumper sticker.

Even so, I got a lot of mileage out of it. Giving after-lunch talks to civic clubs and senior citizen groups, I made ample use of the slogan, which always drew a chorus of guffaws from the longtime Richmonders in the audiences. They understood the slogan was humor laced with a dose of truth.

All cities have experienced hard times.

But anyone with more than a cursory knowledge of Richmond's history knows the city has endured more than its fair share of woe.

Most of Richmond's troubles, yesteryear and today, are directly related to the city's key role in the Civil War, when the city wound up on the wrong side of history. As no one seems to forget, Richmond was the capital of the Confederate States of America—a historical fact that today is both a blessing and a curse.

This status is a blessing in that Richmond is a must-see destination for legions of Civil War history enthusiasts who visit the city each year. It is a curse in that Richmond is still struggling to heal racial wounds directly linked to its Confederate heritage.

ON THE SURFACE, RICHMOND IS AN OLD TOBACCO TOWN. TOBACCO MADE THE CITY PROSPER early on, and tobacco still puts food in a lot of pantries and refrigerators. After all, this is where Philip Morris manufactures Marlboros by the gazillions in one of the world's largest cigarette factories.

The city's trump suit, however, is history. Richmond's story is unique. No other American city can claim to be the place where Patrick Henry gave his "Give me liberty or give me death" speech, where the state capitol was designed by Thomas Jefferson, where Aaron Burr was tried for treason (he was acquitted) in a trial presided over by Chief Justice John

1861
TO
1865

BATTRIES
PURCELL, CRENSHAW,
LETCHER PEE DEE
FREDERICKSBURG
PRESENTED MAY 3RD 1887

Marshall, and where the government of the ill-fated Confederate States of America set up shop during the Civil War.

Is Richmond too enamored of its history? Is the city mired in its bygone years? Do Richmonders spend too much time dwelling on the past, when they should be looking down the road to the future? As we move forward into the 21st century, those legitimate questions are being asked by some critics who say the city is, indeed, too backward-looking.

They argue that Richmond's infatuation with its history is the reason it has been eclipsed by any number of southern cities (Atlanta and Charlotte, for example) that once looked up to Richmond as a preeminent city.

Frankly, there is some truth to the notion that the past tends to hold Richmond back. But Richmond cannot afford to turn its back on its past.

Why? One-word answer: Tourism.

Each year, thousands of tourists from all over the world visit the city. They come here for many reasons, but vast numbers of them come for one reason and one reason only: to soak up the city's colorful past. If Richmond were to stop promoting its history, you could

bet your bottom Confederate dollar that the city would lose a large stack of U.S. dollars.

The main draw is the city's Civil War role, which put Richmond on the map of historically important American cities. Tourists come here to visit the Museum of the Confederacy and the White House of the Confederacy, the home where Confederate President Jefferson Davis lived during the war.

They come to see the new Civil War Visitors Center, operated by the U.S. Park Service, and to tour the battlefields around the city.

They come to visit Hollywood Cemetery, Richmond's most famous burial ground, where Jefferson Davis and thousands of Confederate soldiers are buried, along with two U.S. presidents—James Monroe and John Tyler.

They come to drive along fabled Monument Avenue to look at and photograph the large, impressive equestrian statues of Confederate heroes Robert E. Lee, Jeb Stuart, and Stonewall Jackson.

And they come because they know Richmond was the southern city Abraham Lincoln so desperately wanted to capture. For the Union to be preserved, Lincoln knew Richmond had to fall.

Fall it did, and when it fell, Lincoln came to town. ☛

Historian Harry M. Ward described Lincoln's visit on April 4, 1865, in his book, *Richmond: An Illustrated History*, published in 1985: "At 11 a.m., Richmonders were in for a most unusual surprise—the arrival of the president of the United States. Lincoln had come up [river] in a federal naval flotilla from City Point, where he had conferred with General Grant for several days. Taking his young son, Tad, in tow, and surrounded by 12 sailors with fixed bayonets, Lincoln walked up Main Street. One Richmond woman recalled that the president was the 'ugliest man I ever saw,' and an old black resident said that Lincoln, tanned from being at the outdoor conferences at City Point, looked like 'an ornery old farmer.' "

Rᴄʜᴍᴏɴᴅ ᴘᴀɪᴅ ᴀ ᴅᴇᴀʀ ᴘʀɪᴄᴇ ғᴏʀ ʙᴇɪɴɢ ᴛʜᴇ ᴄᴇɴᴛʀᴀʟ ᴄɪᴛʏ ᴏғ ᴛʜᴇ Cᴏɴғᴇᴅᴇʀᴀᴄʏ's "lost cause." Before the war, Richmond had been one of the nation's most important cities, economically and politically. It was a financial center, an industrial powerhouse, a commercial hub. It also was the capital of Virginia, which at that time wielded tremendous influence in the affairs of the nation.

The city's dominant industry then, as now, was tobacco manufacturing. Millions of pounds of the leaf were produced here each year, and the city's leading tobacconists became fabulously wealthy.

Besides tobacco, antebellum Richmond was a major producer of flour. The city's two leading manufacturers, Gallego Mills and Columbia Mills, were said to be the largest flour mills in the nation. Richmond-made flour was exported to as far away as South America. Other Richmond products in those boom years included iron, cotton cloth, woolen goods, paper, nails, leather, hats, and soap.

In the decade before the Civil War, Richmond became the third most affluent city in the nation, based on per capita income.

There are numerous first-person accounts of Richmonders who lived here during the prewar boom years. In his memoirs written two decades after the war, John Lange, a German immigrant who operated a saloon before, during, and after the war, described antebellum Richmond's prosperity. "The years 1858, 1859, 1860 were flowering years for the city," he wrote. "Who wanted to work could find a job. Wages were high, food was cheap. Houses shot out of the ground like mushrooms."

William Makepeace Thackeray, the English writer, came to Richmond to give a lecture in 1853. The city impressed him. He described it as a "comfortable, friendly, cheery little town"—the most picturesque he had seen in America. ☛

The Civil War put the brakes on the good times.

As the war dragged on for four long years, Richmond became a city under siege by enemy troops. Food became scarce, especially meat. The situation became so desperate that Jefferson Davis suggested that the city's residents catch and eat rats, which, Davis claimed, were just as tasty as squirrels.

Phoebe Yates Pember, a South Carolina woman who came here during the war to care for wounded soldiers, made available to Richmonders her recipe for cooking rats, which could be made palatable if the cook were to "baste with bacon fat and roast before a good fire quickly like canvasback ducks."

When the war ended in April 1865, Richmond was anything but picturesque, as Thackeray had described it 12 years earlier. Most of the city's business district was in ruins, destroyed by fires set by fleeing Confederate troops in what is known as the Evacuation Fire of 1865.

Postwar Richmond, though, was quite a scene.

Federal troops occupied the city, and the city's large supply of prostitutes, who had

done business with Confederate soldiers during the war, now turned their attention to plying their trade with drunken Yankees.

Hordes of civilians, mainly from the North, came to town in hopes of making a quick fortune helping the city to rebuild. And large numbers of freed slaves, many of whom had been field hands in the countryside around Richmond, streamed into the city, swelling the population and creating a social problem.

Yet, Richmond managed to regroup in the postwar years. By the turn of the 20th century, Richmond once again was a vibrant city. Among the major cities in the 11 Old South states that had joined the Confederacy, Richmond was—with the possible exception of Atlanta—the region's preeminent city.

In 1900, Richmond's population was 85,050. Atlanta's was 89,872. By comparison, Charlotte—where aggressive bankers helped to boost the Queen City of the Carolinas into a financial powerhouse in the second half of the 20th century—had a population of just 18,091 when the 20th century began.

Mention of Charlotte always brings back pleasant memories of a newspaper column I wrote in the summer of 1982. The column, an exercise in hyperbole, poked fun at Charlotte, portraying the upstart city as an overgrown truck stop. ☛

To my good fortune, Kays Gary, then a columnist with the *Charlotte Observer*, fired back with a column taking a verbal potshot at Richmond.

Thus began a columnists' duel, which I dubbed the Uncivil War Between Richmond and Charlotte. Over a period of several weeks, Kays and I took turns ridiculing the other's city.

Kays, a great guy who died several years ago, came up with some wonderfully witty lines about Richmond. His best line was one I'll never forget, because it summed up Richmonders' devotion to the past.

Kays wrote, "Richmond is a city in which the people with all the power, all the clout, all the influence, are people who died a long time ago."

Richmond does have a thing about its history, but on the edge of a new century, it is incorrect and unfair to say the city is stuck in the past. The city does not have the financial clout it once had—all its major banks are now headquartered in other cities—but the Richmond area remains economically strong, as proved by its standing as the home to several Fortune 500 companies.

When I moved to Richmond from Atlanta in 1972, it was not love at first sight. After

living in "Hot-Lanta," where a building boom in the 1960s made the skyline change almost daily, I found Richmond's skyline small and dreary. The tallest building was a 20-story bank building.

Today, Richmond's skyline still is no match for Atlanta's, but it has changed dramatically over the past few decades. Driving into the city from the south on Interstate 95, even a motorist from New York City has to admire

the view of Richmond, especially at night.

I also thought Richmond had far too many old buildings when I first arrived in town. I wondered if anything ever was torn down.

It did not take long, however, for me to develop an appreciation for Richmond's abundance of old brick. Thanks to a dedicated group of preservationists, large numbers of grand old buildings that would have been torn down long ago in most cities have been saved from the wrecking ball.

Old City Hall, for example. Built in 1903, this eye-fetching example of Gothic architecture was renovated and converted into an office building in 1972 when a new city hall was built on the other side of Broad Street.

In many cities, a building like Old City Hall would have been demolished to make way for a new building. Not in Richmond. The building was saved, and many Richmonders consider it to be downtown's most attractive building.

Its mixture of old and new architecture is one of Richmond's strongest assets. The diver-

sity of architecture, coupled with the natural beauty of the James River winding its way through the heart of the city on its way to the Chesapeake Bay, is why almost every out-of-towner who comes here is prone to describe Richmond as a beautiful city.

Without question, the James River is a wonderful asset, although it was an asset that tended to flood too often for years. Today, the threat of flooding has virtually disappeared, thanks to a flood wall built in the 1990s by the Army Corps of Engineers.

One of the main benefits of the flood wall is that it has spurred redevelopment in the city's oldest commercial district, Shockoe Bottom. For years, the Bottom's buildings were flooded during major floods. As a result, most of the buildings were vacant eyesores. Thanks to flood control, the Bottom has been rejuvenated. Its old buildings have been turned into restaurants, shops, offices, and apartments. Coupled with the nearby Shockoe Slip commercial district, that area of town has become a popular spot for dining and nightlife.

Richmond's beauty, however, goes much deeper than what one sees on the surface. The city has a certain charm, a certain graciousness about it that is unique to Richmond.

As in all vibrant communities, Richmond's strongest asset is its people.

Given the fact that many Richmonders are descendants of slaves, and that many others are descendants of slave owners and Confederate soldiers, anyone who does not know the city might view it as a racially divided city where whites and blacks are unable to get along.

Not so.

Oh, Richmond has to suffer through an occasional controversy that is racially divisive, but day in and day out, the vast majority of blacks and whites in this city get along. They seem to understand that the past is the past and is gone with the wind.

Still, the past is what makes Richmond interesting.

As the whimsical slogan I suggested some years ago implies, this old Virginia city has seen a lot of troubles. Remarkably, through all the years, Richmond and its people have been blessed with the ability to endure the troubled times, to bounce back, to remake the city, and to move on.

For that reason, those of us who live here are proud to call Richmond home. ★

STRETCHING ALONG THE BANKS
of the James River, Richmond
takes on a tranquil glow in the
light of early morning.

*I*NCORPORATED AND OFFICIALLY deemed Virginia's third capital in 1782, Richmond embraces its rich and complex political heritage. Monument Avenue is lined with statues, most of which portray Confederate officers such as Robert E. Lee (BOTTOM, IN FOREGROUND). Carved homages to George Washington and other founding fathers of the United States greet visitors to Capitol Square (TOP) and the Thomas Jefferson-designed capitol (OPPOSITE).

▲ © DAVID L. EVERETTE

▲ © DAVID L. EVERETTE

On pedestals around the city, Richmond's cast of bronze characters restages regional and national history. Harry Flood Byrd, Virginia senator and governor, stands firm on the capitol's grounds (RIGHT), where George Washington also keeps a firm grip on the reins (OPPOSITE LEFT). On Monument Avenue, tennis star and writer Arthur Ashe brandishes books and a tennis racket (LEFT); several statues to the west is a likeness of Jefferson Davis (OPPOSITE RIGHT), serving as a reminder of Richmond's one-time status as the capital of the Confederate States of America.

G R E A T E R   R I C H M O N D

FROM THE GROUND UP, RICH-mond gleams with the promise fulfilled by its people. Officer Melvin Bond—the city's sole walking-beat policeman (LEFT)—has patrolled the area around City Hall since 1999. In addition to Bond's more standard duties, he serves as a living map of the city, providing directions for residents and visitors.

6TH STREET MARKETPLACE

TIME MAY OCCASIONALLY SEEM to stop in Richmond, but progress never halts. From the Science Museum of Virginia, housed in the historic Broad Street Station (BOTTOM) to the Virginia Commonwealth University campus (TOP), the city dishes up the latest technology.

*I*N A WORLD FULL OF PEOPLE pressed for time, Richmond's businesspeople seize recreational opportunities whenever and wherever it suits them— even if that means substituting a catnap or some high-speed fishing for a power lunch.

GOING WITH THE FLOW: AL Broaddus (ABOVE), president of the Federal Reserve Bank of Richmond, stands at the institution's helm to help it safely navigate the river of high finance. On Brown's Island–along the Canal Walk and within sight of the Federal Reserve–a bronze batteauman (OPPOSITE) is locked in a perpetual battle with the James River. For much of the 19th century, batteaumen performed the dangerous, often thankless task of transporting crops and other goods along the region's waterways.

EVIDENCE OF THE JAMES RIVER'S ongoing, vital role in Richmond's economy is visible almost everywhere in the city. As executive director of the Port of Richmond, located on the west bank of the river, Martin Moynihan (OPPOSITE BOTTOM) oversees the facility, which handles more than 500,000 tons of goods each year. Items passing through the port include everything from vehicles and machinery to forest products and tobacco.

*S*OME MAY FEEL THAT RICH-mond's consistent growth and revitalization are simply the result of hardheadedness. City architects and construction workers, however, know that a lot of brainpower and elbow grease go into the planning, building, or renovating of every structure.

*R*ICHMOND'S HISTORIC RIVER-front area, once a strictly utilitarian part of the city, is now also a popular recreational destination. During the Civil War, the Tredegar Iron Works (ABOVE) manufactured equipment, in-cluding the iron plating for the C.S.S. *Virginia*, for Confederate forces. In its present incarnation as a visitor center, the facility houses three stories' worth of Civil War-era artifacts. Along the James River and Kanawha Canal (OPPOSITE), originally used for shipping goods, visitors can now stroll the 1.5-mile Canal Walk or take advantage of guided boat and walking tours.

*I*N RICHMOND, IT'S NOT THE scale of a job that matters, but the craftsmen's sterling attention to detail. Silversmith Joe Dart has operated the House of Silver (ABOVE) since 1978, restoring metal objects to their original luster for individuals and organizations. ALSTOM Power, one of the city's 50 largest employers (OPPOSITE), produces power generation systems and equipment including gas turbines and steam power plants.

KEEPING AN EAR TO THE
ground: It's easy to hear echoes
of Richmond's history in the
city's present. Each year, Native
American chiefs from regional
tribes make a tribute, in lieu of
taxes, to the Commonwealth's
governor (BOTTOM). At Henricus
Historical Park, living-history
exhibits guide visitors through
a chronology of the area's past.
The Native American portion
of the program includes cooking, pottery, flint knapping, and
other demonstrations (OPPOSITE).

*F*OLKS ENGAGED IN A TUG-OF-war with the rigors of everyday life can take the city up on any of its recreational offerings. At the annual Richmond Highland Games and Celtic Festival (TOP AND OPPOSITE TOP), members of some 50 clans compete in musical, athletic, and other contests. Others may prefer to jet on over to the Virginia Aviation Museum (OPPOSITE BOTTOM), which keeps visitors' heads in the clouds with aircraft including military planes and a vast collection of vintage flying machines.

THE FIGHT IS AFOOT: DAVID Leong (TOP LEFT), chair of the Department of Theatre at Virginia Commonwealth University, has turned his childhood fascination with cinematic swordplay into a lifelong career. As a highly sought-after combat choreographer, Leong has coordinated fight scenes for hundreds of productions worldwide. There's nothing staged about the tension in the works of Richmond playwright Bo Wilson (OPPOSITE). His two-act *War Story* won an award from the Denver Center Theatre and has been optioned for full production.

FROM MOUNTS TO MOTORCYCLES, the Richmond Police Department takes to the streets to protect the populace—and occasionally to pose for the paparazzi. Actor Sir Anthony Hopkins (OPPOSITE BOTTOM) had the city in the palm of his hand during the filming of *Hannibal*, which used various locales in the area. One of Richmond's most well-known modern native sons, Tom Wolfe (OPPOSITE TOP) has produced a small library's worth of articles, essays, and novels since launching his writing career in the early 1960s.

CREATURES OF A FEATHER:
Preserving part of Richmond's
legendary literary heritage, the
Edgar Allan Poe Museum
(ABOVE) has roosted in a section
of the Old Stone House, the city's oldest surviving structure,
since 1922. Fans of Poe's writing
flock to the museum to see exhibits that include a model of
the city during Poe's time, as
well as such artifacts as photo- graphs, daguerreotypes, letters,
and other documents that trace
the author's work and tempestu-
ous personal life.

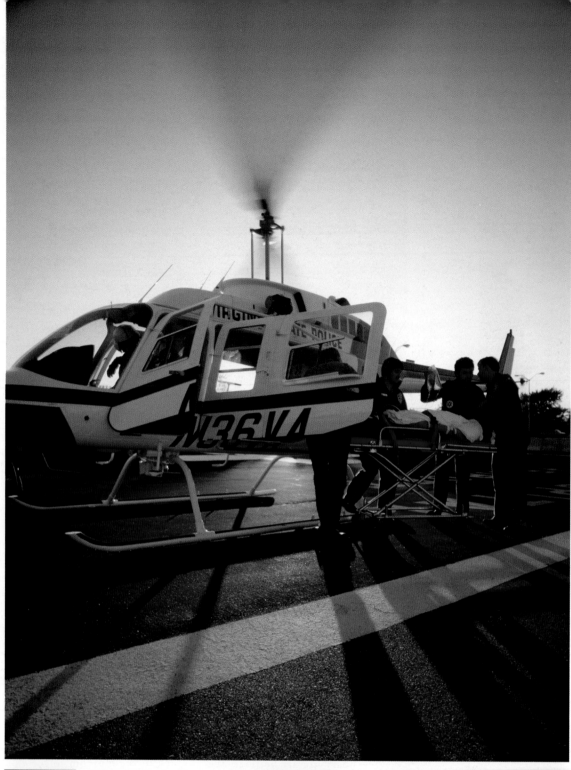

DISASTER STRIKES UNEXPECT-
edly and in a variety of guises.
Whatever the nature of the
crisis, Richmond's emergency
teams respond quickly, whether
by land or by air.

*M*ONUMENTS TO THE DEAD shine a torch on their lives and help keep the flame of their spirits alive in Richmond. The Virginia War Memorial (TOP) honors Virginia natives lost to armed conflict since World War II, much as the Confederate Soldiers Monument (OPPOSITE TOP) remembers those who fell to Union troops. Cofounded by Jay Ipson (BOTTOM) in 1996, the Virginia Holocaust Museum stands as a tribute to those killed in the Holocaust and as an attempt to teach tolerance through education.

CLOAKED IN HUSHED GRANDEUR, Richmond's Hollywood Cemetery provides a peaceful resting place for both the famous— including James Monroe and Jefferson Davis—and the virtually unknown: The cemetery's towering granite pyramid (TOP) memorializes some 18,000 Confederate soldiers. Built in 1741, St. John's Episcopal Church (OPPOSITE) is the oldest church in the city. In 1775, it heard what may have been its most indelible sermon, when Patrick Henry delivered his "Give me liberty or give me death" speech to an electrified audience.

*A*LWAYS FETCHING ATTENTION, dogs provide a window into human nature. The iron will of man's best friend—whether awaiting the huntmaster's call or standing guard over a grave at Hollywood Cemetery—is matched only by the determination of pet owners whose companions have been temporarily misplaced.

As PASTORAL DIRECTOR FOR Richmond Hill, an urban retreat center, the Reverend Benjamin P. Campbell guides attendees through the ups and downs—and periodic stormy weather—of their lives. The facility, which can accommodate as many as 40 people at once, also maintains a chapel, library, and gardens that are open to the public.

WEST OF THE BOULEVARD DE-
fines a residential and commercial section of Richmond rich
in Georgian architecture and
fantastic shopping. Home to
Carytown—a stretch of West
Cary Street lined by some 250
shops and restaurants—the area
incorporates residential properties ranging from apartments
to stately old homes overlooking
the James River.

The Virginia Statute for Religious Freedom

We the General Assembly of Virginia do enact that no man shall be compelled to frequent or support any religious worship, place, or ministry whatsoever, nor shall be enforced, restrained, molested, or burdened in his body or goods, nor shall otherwise suffer on account of his religious opinions or belief; but that all men shall be free to profess, and by argument to maintain, their opinions in matters of religion, and that the same shall in no wise diminish, enlarge, affect their civil capacities. **1786**

Thomas Jefferson

EACH OF RICHMOND'S NEIGH-borhoods has a colorful history that contributes to the spectrum that is the city. Shockoe Bottom (ABOVE), a major industrial center in the 19th century, now enjoys a rehabilitated reputation as an artists' mecca. Slightly west of downtown, the historic Fan district (OPPOSITE TOP) comprises one of the largest intact Victorian neighborhoods in the state.

WORSHIPERS AT TRINITY BAPTIST Church in Richmond have found a great deal to praise since the church was founded in 1906. Pastor A. Lincoln James Jr. (RIGHT), who stepped up to Trinity's pulpit in 1980, ministers to a flock of more than 5,000 members.

OVER THE YEARS, CONTRIBUTIONS made by Richmond's African-American residents have helped steer the course of national history. The Maggie L. Walker National Historic Site (TOP RIGHT)—in the heart of the Jackson Ward district—celebrates the life of the first woman in the country to found and preside over a bank. Jackson Ward is also home to the Black History Museum and Cultural Center of Virginia, which—under the leadership of Executive Director Charles E. Bethea (BOTTOM RIGHT)—holds an ever increasing, permanent collection of records commemorating accomplishments of African-American Virginians. One prominent Richmonder, nationally lauded lawyer and local legend Oliver W. Hill Sr. (OPPOSITE), has been immortalized in a bronze bust displayed at the museum. Hill spent his 60-year career dealing with civil rights issues such as the right of African-Americans to serve as jury members and vote in primaries. One of Hill's cases also became part of the landmark *Brown v. Board of Education* decision. Litigating on the business law front, attorney Robert J. Grey Jr. (BOTTOM LEFT) is a partner in the prestigious Richmond branch of LeClair Ryan and is active in a number of civic and bar associations.

THE DOORS OF OPPORTUNITY IN the historic Jackson Ward district are never really closed. The neighborhood has produced such local civic and professional leaders as the Foster Brothers (TOP, FROM LEFT)—Dr. Francis M. Foster, Kermit M. Foster, Wilbert F. "Skip" Foster, and Richard W. Foster—and has provided a platform for Waverly R. Crawley (BOTTOM), the self-proclaimed mayor of Second Street and ambassador for historic Jackson Ward.

*L*OCAL BUSINESSES HAVE COME and gone throughout the Jackson Ward neighborhood's long history. Shop owners like Hae Joo Kim (BOTTOM RIGHT) of King's Fish continue to reel in customers with their daily spe- cials, and buildings that once housed such establishments as the Richmond Dairy Co. have undergone major changes. The structure gained a new lease on life when it was converted into apartments (OPPOSITE).

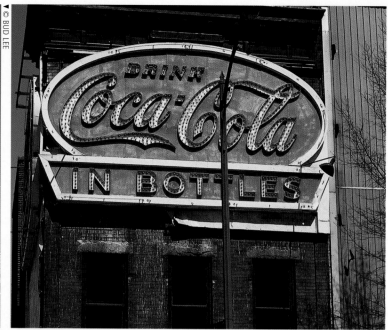

WITH ITS OLD-FASHIONED SIGNS,
abundant restaurants, and shops
to serve every need, Shockoe
Bottom is considered by many
to be a cut above the rest.

PAWNING HISTORY JUST ISN'T AN option. Once a grand welcome for people entering the city by train, the Main Street Station (TOP), built in 1901 and now listed on the National Register of Historic Places, serves as office space as it prepares to resume its original purpose. The Farmers' Market in Shockoe Bottom (OPPOSITE) has been producing a bustling business for more than 200 years, selling a wide variety of fresh fruits and vegetables, cheeses, and flowers.

RICHMOND IS STUFFED WITH A full menu of eateries. Man may not be able to live by bread alone, but Billy Fallen, owner of Billy Bread (TOP), gets all floured up just the same. Local restaurateur and raconteur Jimmy Sneed (BOTTOM) constantly cooks up ideas for new area eateries. In 1989, Paul Keevil opened Millie's Diner (OPPOSITE TOP), which specializes in equally diverse menu and jukebox selections, and the River City Diner's airy Shockoe Bottom location (OPPOSITE BOTTOM) dishes out huge portions of food in its nostalgic 1950s atmosphere.

Keep an eye on the architectural twists and turns all around Richmond. The city's compendium of often-eccentric stylistic blends includes the Egyptian Building (top), built in 1845 at the height of the Egyptian Revival period. The facility is now home to the administrative offices of the Department of Physical Medicine and Rehabilitation at Virginia Commonwealth University's Medical College of Virginia.

SIGNS OF THE SEASON, ICICLES and snow can lend an eerie beauty to Richmond. They're usually short-lived, though: The city's average annual snowfall is notably light, and winter temperatures generally hover around the 40-degree mark.

*H*OLIDAY CHEER TRAVELS QUICK-ly, whether by sleigh or by plane. Ricky Duling, a retired city policeman known to most city residents as Sgt. Santa (OPPOSITE BOTTOM), has made a second ca-reer of collecting and distribut-ing gifts for the disadvantaged. Just seven miles southeast of the city, at Richmond International Airport (OPPOSITE TOP), more than a dozen air carriers light up the sky, transporting nearly 3 million passengers each year.

F OR WORLD TRAVELERS, THE Virginia Museum of Fine Arts (LEFT) offers thousands of years of human expression spanning five continents. Recently renovated and renamed the Richmond Landmark Theater, the building formerly known as The Mosque (OPPOSITE TOP) was built by Shriners in the 1920s and has been a city-owned performing arts venue since 1940. The Carpenter Center for the Performing Arts (OPPOSITE BOTTOM)— designed as a cinema during the golden age of movies—now seats more than 2,000 patrons for performances by organizations such as the Richmond Symphony Orchestra, Richmond Ballet, and Virginia Opera.

RICHMOND-BASED ARTISTS USE the canvases of their experience to portray a full range of perspectives. Muralist Happy Kuhn (TOP) has been wielding a whimsical brush for most of his life, producing images of politicians and animals with equal aplomb. Paul DiPasquale (OPPOSITE TOP, ON RIGHT) creates public sculptures that illustrate history-making people and events. His ever expanding list of projects includes a bust of Richmond civic leader and historian Mary Tyler Cheek McClenahan (OPPOSITE TOP, ON LEFT). Dr. W. Baxter Perkinson Jr. (OPPOSITE BOTTOM) has cut his professional teeth on two successful careers—dentistry and watercolor painting. All proceeds from his art are donated to various causes.

Vaudevillian Bill "Bojangles" Robinson, born in Richmond's Jackson Ward district in 1878, went on to tap-dance his way into the hearts of fans across the country. Robinson maintained close ties with his hometown, and eventually donated a much-needed traffic light to Jackson Ward. A statue near the light stands as another reminder of the performer's generosity (OPPOSITE). Just a few steps from Jackson Ward, the Carpenter Center (BOTTOM LEFT) celebrates all varieties of performing arts.

DURING SOME SPRING AND summer holidays, hats seem to blossom on the heads of area residents parading down the streets. Those who choose to go bareheaded may pull strings to have others don headgear.

IF LIFE IS A MOVIE, THE PRO-
ducers may wish to consider
shopping for props, wardrobe,
and extras in Richmond. The
city's ethnic celebrations,
including the Irish Festival
(ABOVE) and Greek Festival

(OPPOSITE, BOTTOM RIGHT) give
residents a chance to indulge in
traditional dances and costumes.
At Showcase, a 60,000-square-
foot store housed in the old
Pohlig Brothers warehouse on
Church Hill (OPPOSITE, TOP AND

BOTTOM LEFT), shoppers can
dance to any beat they wish.
The massive establishment sells
everything from life-size manne-
quins and other collectibles to
furniture and store fixtures.

Music fills the air in Richmond, whether it's used to entertain, to explore one's roots, or simply to take a break from the rest of the day. The yearly Richmond Children's Festival serves as an instrument for featuring area musicians and other artists (OPPOSITE TOP). Members of the Elegba Folklore Society educate their audiences through artistically oriented events like the Down Home Family Reunion (OPPOSITE, BOTTOM RIGHT), which attracts nearly 25,000 people annually.

MUSIC-MAKERS OF NOTE ABOUND in the Richmond area. John Crouch of J.W. Crouch painstakingly crafts made-to-order guitars and mandolins in his Mechanicsville workshop (TOP). Standards in the city's music scene for decades, local favorites George Winn and the Bluegrass Partners perform regularly at establishments such as Poe's Pub (BOTTOM). Putting their money where customers' mouths are, German manufacturer Hohner introduced the harmonica to North America in 1862: The company's Richmond branch now produces more than 90 kinds of harmonicas (OPPOSITE).

*A*PPLAUSE, PLEASE: THE MEMBERS of the Kevin Gaines Quintet (TOP RIGHT) inspire Richmond audiences with their one-of-a-kind sound. Singer-songwriter Susan Greenbaum (OPPOSITE), a former Fortune 500 company executive, has opted for life on the stage instead of in the boardroom.

*I*T'S CALLED THE BIG GIG FOR A reason. From classic acts such as the Temptations (TOP) to classical groups like the Richmond Concert Band (BOTTOM LEFT), music of every possible era and genre sounds off at the annual July event. The multiweek concert features performances— many of them free—at varied locales and draws tens of thousands of music lovers.

*R*ICHMOND'S CITYWIDE STUDENT Harp Ensemble (ABOVE) is the first program of its kind in the nation. Participants, many of whom serve as mentors for their academic peers, frequently perform in local settings, including hospitals and nursing homes. The Richmond Ballet (OPPOSITE), founded in the 1950s as a civic organization, became Virginia's only professional ballet company
in 1984. The troupe stages its pointedly praised programs for some 50,000 people around the Commonwealth.

SIGNS OF LOVE MAKE THEMSELVES known throughout Richmond: The city itself constitutes an uncanny marriage of ideals and historic romance.

Kids are people too: Getting new residents off to a healthy start is a Richmond priority. Children's Hospital, a specialty pediatric facility that began life as a free clinic in 1917, offers services that range from dental and feeding programs to orthopedics, as well as the region's first transitional care unit.

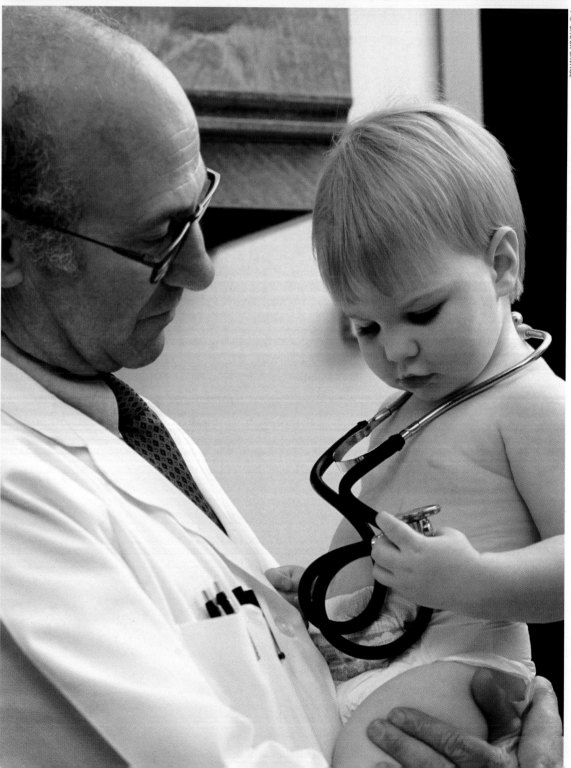

*I*T'S A BEAUTIFUL DAY IN NEIGH-borhoods of all ages, sizes, and styles in Richmond. From the late-19th-century Victorian Dooley Estate at Maymont Park (BOTTOM LEFT AND OPPOSITE, BOTTOM LEFT) to established communities and new residential construction, the city houses nearly 200,000 residents within the shelter of its welcoming walls.

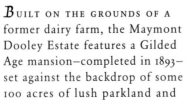

Built on the grounds of a former dairy farm, the Maymont Dooley Estate features a Gilded Age mansion–completed in 1893–set against the backdrop of some 100 acres of lush parkland and gardens. The estate was bequeathed to the city in 1925, and visitors are now free to tour the house and grounds. Native Virginia wildlife such as bison, hawks, and red foxes roam the park's outdoor animal exhibits; Maymont also contains a nature center, aviary, and children's farm, and plays host each year to numerous concert series, festivals, and other events.

GREATER RICHMOND

*D*IVING INTO THE RICHMOND area's natural beauty and opportunities for relaxation can be a breathtaking experience. The city is awash in private pools, and the Department of Parks, Recreation and Community Facilities maintains nearly a dozen public swimming pools as well.

THE BRIDGES THAT SPAN THE James River serve cars, pedestrians, and the occasional daredevil. Belle Isle, a 60-acre island in the middle of the river, is accessible via the Robert E. Lee Bridge (OPPOSITE), which offers a suspended walkway in addition to its paved surface.

THE JAMES RIVER STILL PLAYS an important part in everyday life for people like fisherman Mickey Hopkins (BOTTOM) and world-renowned recording artists Donna Meade and Jimmy Dean (OPPOSITE BOTTOM), area residents who live near the river's edge and are highly vocal in their efforts to help preserve the waterway. The annual James River Batteau Festival makes waves with its eight-day, 120-mile journey (OPPOSITE TOP), which parallels the route undertaken by the batteaumen who once navigated the river to transport goods. The event emphasizes the James River as a natural resource and encourages the building of batteau replicas.

*R*OLLING ON THE RIVER—or simply lounging on its banks and taking in the view—provides endless amusement for the region's residents and visitors alike. Popular white-water spots include the Hollywood Rapids at Belle Isle (TOP AND OPPOSITE BOTTOM) and the Pipeline Rapid near Brown's Island (BOTTOM).

FROM ANY ANGLE, RICHMOND and its surrounds provide plenty of outlets for athletes and thrill seekers. Richmond served as one of two 1999 locations for the annual ESPN X Trials (TOP), which feature hundreds of athletes from around the world competing for medals and prize money. At Paramount's King's Dominion (OPPOSITE BOTTOM), 20 miles north of the city, attendees can choose from a palace's worth of rides and attractions, including 11 roller coasters and the Water-Works water park.

FIELD GOALS: SPORTS OF EVERY kind make a hit in Richmond, although some would-be participants may get teed off when the ball proves too heavy to lift.

THE RACE IS ON: SOMETIMES IT'S the speed, not the species, that determines survival of the fittest. Located about a half-hour's drive from Richmond, Colonial Downs (BOTTOM RIGHT) is right on track when it comes to Thoroughbred and harness racing. At the annual State Fair of Virginia, the pig races hog all the attention while they're in progress (OPPOSITE BOTTOM). And, on the human front, triathletes do their multitalented best to leave the competition behind.

*G*O, SPEED RACER: RICHMOND International Raceway (LEFT) fills up for a full range of contests, including the NASCAR Winston Cup Series, which it has hosted since 1953. Getting up on a soapbox is a natural for some young drivers-in-training (OPPOSITE BOTTOM), and other folks prove that growing older has nothing to do with slowing down (OPPOSITE TOP).

𝒜 NATIVE RICHMONDER AND NASCAR Winston Cup Series veteran, Junie Donlavey has paid his toll to the racing world since 1949. As owner of Donlavey Racing and the No. 90 Hills Bros Coffee Ford Taurus, he has garnered a vast collection of achievements, and more than a dozen of his team members are listed among NASCAR's 50 greatest drivers.

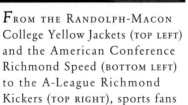

*F*ROM THE RANDOLPH-MACON College Yellow Jackets (TOP LEFT) and the American Conference Richmond Speed (BOTTOM LEFT) to the A-League Richmond Kickers (TOP RIGHT), sports fans get a kick out of their local athletic teams. The Richmond Renegades (BOTTOM RIGHT) began playing in the East Coast Hockey League in 1990 and iced the competition, taking home the team's first Riley Cup in 1995. As the Triple-A affiliate of the Atlanta Braves, the Richmond Braves (OPPOSITE) have gone to bat for their hometown at the Diamond since 1985.

*A*LL THE WORLD'S A STAGE IN Richmond, where audiences of all stripes can find a lion's share of entertainment. At the nonprofit Theatre IV (TOP), children's plays are the specialty of the house; musicals shine in the limelight of the historic Swift Creek Mill Playhouse (BOTTOM), housed in a former grist mill that was built in 1655.

FROM THE FIRST SIGN OF THE changing season to the final drifting leaf, autumn in the Richmond region provides a canopy of color that hovers within the grasp of all who would hold onto it.

Since it first opened in the historic Broad Street Station in 1977, the Science Museum of Virginia has been mystifying and edifying guests with a mind-bending array of exhibits. In 2000, the museum held a ceremony to mark the unveiling of its triple-gallery Bioscape, an interactive exploration of the life sciences. The celebration's guests included Bill Nye the Science Guy (RIGHT)—a man who needs no introduction—novelist Patricia Cornwell (OPPOSITE, TOP RIGHT), and Dr. Marcella Fierro (OPPOSITE, TOP LEFT), the medical examiner who inspired the main character for Cornwell's best-selling Kay Scarpetta series.

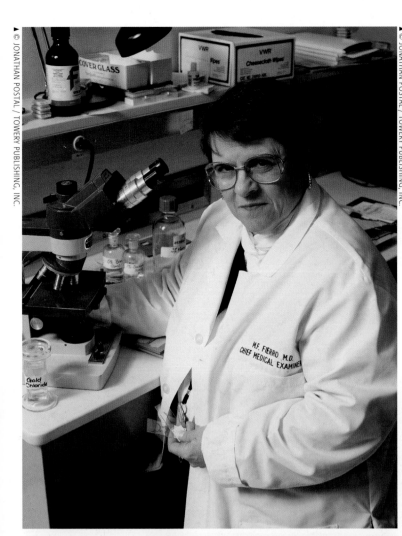

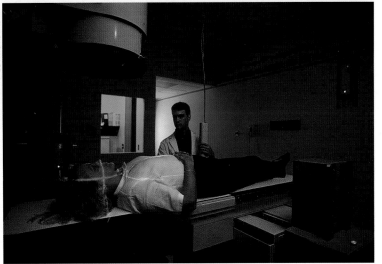

*T*HOUGH SOME MAY VIEW ALL scientific progress as hot air, others see it in a different light. Electric automobiles—recharged by solar panels and on display at the Science Museum of Virginia (OPPOSITE)—represent the new wave in cars. In the medical community, use of such equipment and techniques as electron microscopes and radiation therapy help monitor and improve patients' quality of life (BOTTOM).

CONSIDER THE SCULPTURES OF the field: Sprawling over more than 15 acres, the Lewis Ginter Botanical Garden (OPPOSITE) blooms with a bewildering array of flowers, shrubs, trees, wild- life—and exquisitely carved wooden insects, perhaps the pets of the rough-hewn figures at the Maymont Dooley Estate (ABOVE).

WITH ITS SOARING ARCHITEC-
ture and its agricultural prowess,
its proximity to the majestic
James River, and its acknowledg-
ment of the area's role in history and the part it will play in
the future, Greater Richmond
evokes the promise of a region
on the rise (PAGES 146-153).

1830   Randolph-Macon College

1830   University of Richmond

1850   Richmond Times-Dispatch

1860   GRTC

1865   Bank of America

1877   HCA Richmond Hospitals

1877   Northwestern Mutual Financial Network

1882   Owens & Minor

1895   The Jefferson Hotel

1897   PricewaterhouseCoopers LLP

1897   Schwarzschild Jewelers

1901   Hunton & Williams

Randolph-Macon College

RANDOLPH-MACON COLLEGE, WITH ITS LEGACY NOW EXTEND-
ing to some 175 years, has earned a place among the nation's top liberal arts and sciences colleges. With a strong faculty, sound curriculum, picturesque campus, and student body composed of bright young people, the college has established itself as a place where students enjoy a high-quality undergraduate experience. ⟐ Founded by Methodists in 1830,

Randolph-Macon has a record for attracting and educating students who go on to successful careers in business, law, politics, medicine, education, religion, and the arts. The college's extensive liberal arts curriculum offers 30 majors; an ever-expanding study abroad program; internships with some of the nation's top businesses; an extraordinary undergraduate research program; independent study options; an honors program; and interdisciplinary majors that ensure that each student's education is individualized and varied.

The Best of the Old and the New

Randolph-Macon's 1,100 students also enjoy personal attention, small classes taught exclusively by professors, and opportunities to participate in a full range of activities–from sports to publications to student government. Students also benefit from an active, widespread alumni network that can open doors and provide opportunities. The college is ranked as a national liberal arts college by *U.S. News & World Report*, and is classified as a Baccalaureate 1 institution by the Carnegie Foundation.

Located in Ashland, Virginia, Randolph-Macon's 60 major buildings are set on a classic college campus in a beautiful, small town. Within just a

few minutes of walking time, students can get from any one building to another, or stroll into town to enjoy shopping and dining options.

The school's small-town ambience is complemented by its location just 15 miles from Richmond and 90 miles from Washington, D.C. Both cities offer a wealth of cultural, educational, and recreational opportunities, and both are easily accessible by car or through Ashland's Amtrak station.

Randolph-Macon students compete in the NCAA Division III level in the Old Dominion Athletic Conference. Men's and women's teams have achieved success in a variety of sports. Men's sports include baseball, basketball, football, lacrosse, golf, soccer,

and tennis. Women's sports include basketball, field hockey, lacrosse, soccer, softball, swimming, tennis, and volleyball.

State-of-the-Art Facilities

Randolph-Macon's campus facilities include the McGraw-Page Library, which contains some 175,000 print volumes, music CDs, videos, and microforms; the Flippo Gallery, where the work of students, faculty, and visiting artists is exhibited; Keeble Observatory, which offers public viewing sessions; the Brock Sports and Recreation Center; the Center for Counseling and Career Planning; and the Jordan Wheat Lambert Historic Campus, which includes three buildings listed on the National Register of Historic Places.

An extensive cultural arts program at Randolph-Macon showcases student talent and brings top performers, lecturers, and authors to the campus throughout the year.

Perhaps the most valuable resource Randolph-Macon College has to offer is its faculty. Whether helping students in the classroom, the laboratory, the library, or the greater community, the college's faculty and staff take time to get to know the young people who have come to the campus to achieve an extraordinary, beneficial educational experience.

RANDOLPH-MACON COLLEGE, WITH ITS LEGACY NOW EXTENDING TO SOME 175 YEARS, HAS EARNED A PLACE AMONG THE NATION'S TOP LIBERAL ARTS AND SCIENCES COLLEGES.

FOUNDED IN 1830, THE UNIVERSITY OF RICHMOND IS A PRIVATE, highly selective institution of higher education enrolling some 3,500 full-time students in liberal arts, business, leadership studies, and law programs. Ranked by *U.S. News & World Report* and other college guides as one of the nation's top universities, Richmond has a rising national and international profile. ⁓ The University of Richmond offers students the intimacy of a small college with the range and diversity of a major university. Located

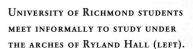

six miles west of downtown, the university's beautiful campus provides an inspirational setting and an extraordinary quality of life for faculty, staff, and students. Its endowment of more than $1 billion and ambitious strategic plan provide strong momentum for the university's future growth and development.

The University of Richmond offers undergraduate degree programs in the arts and sciences, business, and leadership studies. The university also includes highly regarded graduate programs in law and business, as well as master's programs in the arts and sciences. As a testament to the university's selectivity, SAT scores for entering freshmen at Richmond rank in the top 10 percent nationally.

A Sense of Community
The university moved from downtown Richmond to its current west end location in 1914. In 1969, the E. Claiborne Robins family gave the university a transforming gift of $50 million, then the largest gift in the history of higher education; and, in 1987, Robert S. Jepson Jr. and his wife, Alice, gave the university $20 million to launch the nation's first school of leadership studies. The university's endowment currently ranks in the top 40 of all colleges and universities in America.

Through the university, the Richmond community has access to top-notch MBA, law, and graduate programs, certificate and associate's degrees, noncredit classes, career counseling, and customized training for organizations and corporations. The university also contributes to the community by offering programs such as legal clinics and service projects that place bright, highly motivated students in jobs assisting people who need their help.

In addition, the university garnered national attention as host of one of the televised presidential debates in October 1992, and its men's basketball teams have earned a reputation as giant killers, beating Indiana and Syracuse in the 1980s and 1990s.

The Richmond Quest Challenge
In 1999, President William E. Cooper launched a campuswide challenge called the Richmond Quest, which has attracted national attention. Every two years, the University of Richmond's students, staff, and faculty focus their collective attention on a broad and pervasive question that confronts the academy and contemporary society. Beyond seeking an answer to this question, the purpose of the challenge is to explore intellectual connections, thereby strengthening the sense of community across many disciplines.

While rooted in the historic city of Richmond, the University of Richmond prides itself on a tradition of innovation and an unwavering commitment to student-centered learning.

UNIVERSITY OF RICHMOND STUDENTS MEET INFORMALLY TO STUDY UNDER THE ARCHES OF RYLAND HALL (LEFT).

STUDENTS WALK TO CLASS WITH BOATWRIGHT MEMORIAL LIBRARY IN THE BACKGROUND. BOATWRIGHT IS ONE OF FOUR LIBRARIES ON THE UNIVERSITY OF RICHMOND CAMPUS. TOGETHER, THEIR COLLECTIONS EXCEED 1 MILLION ITEMS (RIGHT).

TWO STUDENTS ENJOY THE SPRING WEATHER WHILE WALKING PAST THE BEAUTIFUL STAINED GLASS WINDOW OF CANNON MEMORIAL CHAPEL (LEFT).

A SMALL CLASS MEETS IN STERN QUADRANGLE IN FRONT OF JEPSON HALL. THIS BUILDING, COMPLETED IN 1992, HOUSES THE JEPSON SCHOOL OF LEADERSHIP STUDIES, THE FIRST UNDERGRADUATE LEADERSHIP SCHOOL IN THE NATION (MIDDLE).

STUDENTS HOLD A REVIEW SESSION IN A STUDY LOUNGE IN JEPSON HALL (RIGHT).

ℛ

IN TODAY'S COMPETITIVE, FAST-PACED MEDIA MARKETPLACE, where technology and trends often supplant careful reporting and clear writing, the *Richmond Times-Dispatch* has maintained the principles that have served the newspaper and its readers well through the years. With the recent celebration of the *Times-Dispatch*'s 150th anniversary, the paper recommitted itself to Richmond and to professionalism. ⬙ In a special

anniversary edition, J. Stewart Bryan III, publisher, wrote to readers, "The bottom line is that we still believe—and believe strongly—that tomorrow's educated consumers will continue, for the foreseeable future, to want accurate, fair, understandable accounts of what's going on around them."

Reliable Information in a Complex World

The newspaper's commitment to fulfilling the public's desire for information can be traced to its earliest days. Nine hundred hand-set copies first arrived on the city's streets on October 19, 1850. James A. Cowardin was publisher.

But it was the clamor for reliable information during the Civil War that sent the *Dispatch*'s circulation soaring. During the war, the paper became Richmond's largest, and by the war's end, circulation was more than 30,000. The next century and a half would see a series of mergers and consolidations that created the *Times-Dispatch* of today. Among them was the merger in 1903 with Joseph Bryan's *Daily Times*, which placed the paper in the hands of the family that still operates the paper today, and the 1992 consolidation of the *Times-Dispatch* and *The Richmond News Leader*, Richmond's afternoon paper.

Today, the *Times-Dispatch*, known as Virginia's News Leader, covers central Virginia and much of the state with an editorial staff of approximately 200 writers, editors, photographers, artists, and support personnel in Richmond and in bureaus around the state.

The integrity of the *Times-Dispatch* has not gone unnoticed. In recognition of its skillful news coverage, Virginia Press Association granted the paper its highest award for journalistic integrity and community service twice during the 1990s.

High Standards for the Community

In the last decade, Richmond has begun a regional renaissance, with population and commercial booms in the suburbs, and revitalization of the inner city's neighborhoods and business centers. Concurrently, the *Times-Dispatch* has undergone what Louise C. Seals, managing editor, calls "a sea change" in its culture. The paper is increasingly responding to what readers want to know, as it increasingly reflects the community's diversity.

The technology revolution also has had an impact. Since 1992, the company has cranked out the paper from computerized presses at its plant in Hanover County. Pages designed electronically are dispatched digitally to the plant from the downtown newsroom. News has been featured on a Web site since 1995.

And that newsroom, along with most administrative offices, is located in a new, modern building, the product of a $73 million renovation that has become a cornerstone to downtown Richmond's revitalization. The *Times-Dispatch*'s building is across the street from its parent Media General Corporation's new headquarters building, and near another company project that will bring together broadcast, print, and Internet operations.

"We have 150 years of expertise in providing useful information," says William H. Millsaps Jr., executive editor. "We will adhere to the highest standards. We will be centered—and we will serve the entire community of Richmond and central Virginia. It's not only the proper ethical way to go, it's good business."

SINCE 1850, THE *Richmond Times-Dispatch* HAS BEEN DEDICATED TO SERVING THE NEEDS OF THE CITIZENS OF RICHMOND AND VIRGINIA.

MASAAKI OKADA

MASAAKI OKADA

MASAAKI OKADA

Every day, when the GRTC Transit System sends out its fleet of buses, vans, and trolleys, the company is showing off a little bit of American history. In essence, the buses and vans that make up the GRTC fleet are rolling monuments to the history of mass transportation in the United States. Established in August 1860 with four horse-drawn cars that carried passengers along two routes in the city proper, the transit

company holds the distinction of being the country's first mass transportation system, its officials say.

Since those days, the scope of GRTC's services has changed with the expansion and population growth of the Richmond metropolitan area. Incorporated in 1973, GRTC has been transformed from its earliest horse-and-cart days through various technologies and operating structures. In the late 1880s, the company opened its first electric rail line with six cars, which carried passengers through the capital city until 1949, when the rail was replaced by buses.

Today, the company operates as a nonprofit service corporation jointly owned by the City of Richmond and Chesterfield County. Its fleet includes 164 air-conditioned buses, 111 vans, and eight trolleys that carry passengers along

61 separate routes. This variety of vehicles reflects GRTC's more than a one-size-fits-all approach to serving its customers.

Providing Specialized Services to Area Commuters

With an operating budget that exceeds $20 million, GRTC provides a host of services for riders with special needs. The company's vans and buses are equipped to provide easier boarding and exiting for people with disabilities. Specially equipped GRTC vans also provide curb-to-curb service for people with other considerations, such as wheelchairs or medical equipment.

The company, which employs more than 500 workers, offers other specialized programs, such as charter service and welfare-to-work transportation.

As the Richmond metropolitan area continues to grow, it faces new transportation challenges caused by increasing population and traffic. To help meet this growing demand for transportation, GRTC has begun to make some significant changes to its business and its services. In the near future, GRTC will be constructing a new facility on its existing location on South Davis Avenue in Richmond's Fan District, according to company officials.

Growing to Accommodate Growth

In the meantime, GRTC is making plans to provide more routes beyond its existing service areas in Henrico and Chesterfield counties. And to accommodate a growing number of professionals who depend on GRTC for their work commutes, the company is adding various Park & Ride locations.

In providing more than 10 million customer trips a year, GRTC tries to keep its focus on the basics of mass transit. That means giving its customers a ride that's safe, clean, reliable, and comfortable. Of course, whether they know it or not, GRTC Transit System's customers are getting a little something more for their fare. They're taking a ride through history.

SINCE 1860, GRTC TRANSIT SYSTEM HAS BEEN SAFELY AND EFFICIENTLY SERVING THE PEOPLE OF GREATER RICHMOND. THE SYSTEM'S FLEET INCLUDES 164 AIR-CONDITIONED BUSES, 111 VANS, AND EIGHT TROLLEYS THAT CARRY PASSENGERS ALONG 61 SEPARATE ROUTES.

WHEN BANK OF AMERICA CAME TO RICHMOND IN 1998, IT brought the services, expertise, and clout that only the largest bank in the United States could bring. While clients across the spectrum from individuals to major corporations have benefited from its presence, Bank of America has brought much more to the community. Through a variety of initiatives, it has provided opportunities for small businesses,

prospective home owners, communities seeking restoration, and people who want to improve themselves.

The senior banking executive for Bank of America in Richmond, G.S. "Sandy" Fitz-Hugh Jr., says that through its work, the bank is "leveraging our capabilities and expertise in order to build stronger, healthier neighborhoods."

New Citizen, Long History

Though the Bank of America name is relatively new to Richmond, there are deep banking roots upon which it has been established. Tracing these roots, the bank's origins run back to 1865

when the First National Bank of Richmond was founded. Mergers and acquisitions over time led to 1998, when NationsBank and Bank of America merged and Bank of America took its place in the Richmond marketplace.

With more than $656 billion in total assets, Bank of America has full-service operations in 21 states and the District of Columbia, providing financial services to 30 million households and 2 million businesses.

Bank of America's Richmond area operations are based in the Bank of America Center, a high-rise office tower at 12th and Main streets in the heart of the city's financial district. The com-

pany employs approximately 3,500 people.

Community Development

Bank of America's 10-year, $350 billion national community development lending and investment commitment includes funds for small businesses, affordable housing, economic development, and consumer loans. More than $244 million had been brought to Richmond and the surrounding region when Bank of America announced in 2000 its first-year results of the initiative that quickly identified it as a valuable corporate citizen.

The success of the commitment's first year brought $153 million for affordable housing in Richmond, including loans, investments, and mortgages; $56 million in small business lending; and $35 million in consumer loans. The consumer loans included loans for borrowers with an annual household income at or below 80 percent of the region's median income. Economic development in the Richmond area received $266,000, including loans to and investments in community development financial institutions and venture funds.

The Highland Park Restoration and Preservation Program, which seeks to revitalize the Highland Park area, has received contributions from the bank by way of a credit line and other numerous services. The bank has assisted a "low-income" credit union, which operates from a neighborhood church providing below-market interest rate loans, and financial support has been given to the Richmond Local Initiatives Support Corporation, which provides technical training and support to community development corporations.

Bank of America's Mid-Atlantic Community Development Banking Market Manager Charles R. Henderson Jr. says, "We have an unmatched capacity to deliver these products and to make a positive impact in the communities where we do business."

THOUGH THE BANK OF AMERICA NAME IS RELATIVELY NEW TO RICHMOND, THERE ARE DEEP BANKING ROOTS UPON WHICH IT HAS BEEN ESTABLISHED.

In metropolitan Richmond and the Tri-Cities, HCA Richmond Hospitals collectively provide virtually every health care service conceivable, from primary care to transplants and everything in between. Just as important, they are deeply committed to being good community citizens, responsive to needs beyond their four walls. HCA Richmond Hospitals extend their influence in the community in many ways. Generous in their support of charitable causes, they provide thousands of health screenings throughout the area through their Health Drive team and work in creative ways with dozens of organizations. Whether it's packing blizzard bags for Meals on Wheels, joining the Virginia Department of Health to immunize school children, or walking to raise money for the Heart Association or Cancer Society, HCA and its employees stay involved. And HCA Hospitals are healthy taxpayers, too, paying $60 million in a typical year.

Meeting Community Needs

Today, each of HCA Richmond's six hospitals offers a different mix of services. Yet all are bound by a common mission: a commitment to the care and improvement of human life. While focused on ensuring that each patient leaves the hospital with the best possible clinical outcome, HCA's caregivers also understand the importance of an encouraging word, a gentle touch, and a sympathetic ear. At HCA, technology is paired with compassion and empathy.

More Than Medicine

"Health care is our target, but our definition for health care is broad," says Carolyn Cuthrell, community services manager. "We are a substantial presence in the community, and we work hard at contributing to the community's health and well-being."

In a unique partnership with the Presbyterian School of Christian Education, HCA supports the Caring Congregation program through which nurses marry their professional and spiritual lives. These nurses, many of whom work at HCA hospitals, serve as a resource to their congregations by providing health education, referrals to community services, advocacy and spiritual support.

HCA also financially supports Noah's Children, a children's hospice. And it has made a $300,000 contribution to the Science Museum of Virginia to fund a van that travels to schools statewide, teaching children the mysteries of science and health. This contribution will also make possible the creation of a permanent neurosciences exhibit at the museum.

As Greater Richmond grows, so too will HCA, in a manner consistent with its role as the region's health care leader. That role comes with obligations that each hospital, and the network as a whole, is prepared to meet.

"This is an organization passionate about keeping its heart and its head in the right place," says Marilyn Tavenner, president, HCA Central Atlantic Division. "We spend our resources not just on patients, but on people—whether they're in our hospitals or in our community."

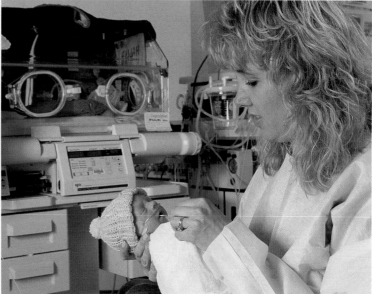

In metropolitan Richmond and the Tri-Cities, HCA Richmond Hospitals collectively provide virtually every health care service conceivable, from primary care to transplants and everything in between.

In 1877, 12 years after the end of the Civil War, a Richmond civic leader opened a local office representing a Wisconsin life insurance company. Considering the times, Colonel John B. Cary must have been crazy to think a northern company could succeed in the South. Many of his contemporaries thought so, and at first he was widely ridiculed. But, in the 20-year-old Northwestern Mutual Life

Insurance Company, Cary saw something unique. He saw a company of unmatched quality and integrity, and he confidently built a thriving business for Northwestern Mutual in Virginia.

Today, more than 120 years later, Cary would still recognize the way the company does business, even though the name is a little different: The Virginia Offices of The Northwestern Mutual Financial Network. The network and its financial representatives form a financial services group anchored by Northwestern Mutual— "The Quiet Company."

The Virginia Offices of The Northwestern Mutual Financial Network is one of the largest and most successful financial services groups in the state, due largely to its financial representatives' ability to help people and businesses successfully define and reach their financial goals, both offensively and defensively.

"When it comes to financial security, we all have different definitions, but we also have one thing in com-

mon—we all want it," says John F. Van Der Hyde, managing director for the Northwestern Mutual Financial Network in the Virginia area. "Our mission as financial representatives is to have our clients finish strong, no matter what their goals."

A Vision for the Future

At Northwestern Mutual Financial Network, the financial representatives first look at the client's vision of his or her future. It says a lot about the client. And like the individual client, each vision is unique. Northwestern's approach involves helping the client shape this vision and attain it. As Van Der Hyde states, "Our mission is to secure your family's future, to make your life better, and to protect what's important to you. You bring us your vision, and we help make it happen."

To accomplish this, the group starts by discussing a client's financial and personal situation, analyzing his or her needs, and focusing on how he or she can make dreams come to life.

Only by doing so can the company help clients plan and prepare for the future. The representatives at the Northwestern Mutual Financial Network develop plans, as well as the means to implement them. "We build an enduring, trusting relationship with our clients so that we are there throughout the different stages of their lives, reassessing their needs as they change, always keeping their original vision in sight," says Van Der Hyde.

Enduring Relationships

Today, the Northwestern Mutual Financial Network provides sound, effective personal planning and advice to its clients throughout the area. The company's representatives are dedicated to providing expert guidance and innovative solutions to help their clients identify and meet financial goals at different stages in their lives.

The group's financial representatives work closely with the Network's trusted financial specialists in areas like retirement planning, estate planning, investment planning, long-term care, insurance planning, and small-business planning to ensure that the needs of a client are examined from every perspective. "This personalized approach leads to customized recommendations that will help you make decisions that are right for you and those who depend on you," Van Der Hyde remarks.

The group's financial representatives offer exclusive access to insurance products and an array of investment choices from Northwestern Mutual, a company that has always received the highest possible financial ratings. In addition, The Northwestern Mutual Financial Network's sales force has been named the best sales force in America by *Sales & Marketing Management* magazine, as well as the number one sales force in the life insurance industry each year the company has been included in the magazine's survey. This recognition is based on sales performance during the previous three

SINCE 1877, NORTHWESTERN MUTUAL FINANCIAL NETWORK HAS BEEN AN INTEGRAL PART OF THE RICHMOND COMMUNITY.

THE NORTHWESTERN MUTUAL FINAN-
CIAL NETWORK PROVIDES FINANCIAL
SOLUTIONS FOR ASSET AND INCOME
PROTECTION, INVESTMENT SERVICES,
PERSONAL PLANNING, EDUCATION
FUNDING, BUSINESS PLANNING, EM-
PLOYEE AND EXECUTIVE BENEFITS,
ESTATE PLANNING, AND RETIREMENT
SOLUTIONS.

years, reputation for customer satisfaction, and interviews with industry analysts and exectives.

Commitment

For the Northwestern Mutual Financial Network, commitment is one of the foundations upon which the group's business is built. Van Der Hyde explains, "When you become a client, you make a financial commitment to those you care about, and you place your trust in us to help make your plans a reality. We appreciate and recognize the significance of that commitment, and we honor it with a commitment of our own: to place your needs and desires first."

Representatives of the Northwestern Mutual Financial Network carry out this commitment by conducting a thorough assessment of a client's needs and matching these needs with the best possible planning strategies and solutions. During this process, each client has exclusive access to the expert guidance and innovative financial solutions available only to network clients. In providing this service, the group's representatives help to protect what is important to most people: securing their futures and improving their lives.

The Virginia Offices of The Northwestern Mutual Financial Network has grown dramatically through the years. Its growth is a testament to a masterful blend of innovative thinking and adherence to core Virginia and company values. The group and its people seek quality over quantity, and integrity above all. The company is in business only to serve the best long-term interests of its clients, helping them plan for their future while they enjoy their present. These values are not new ideas discovered through focus groups and marketing surveys; they are the continuation of Colonel John B. Cary's timeless vision.

JOHN F. VAN DER HYDE IS MANAGING
DIRECTOR OF THE VIRGINIA OFFICES
OF THE NORTHWESTERN MUTUAL
FINANCIAL NETWORK.

Owens & Minor

Owens & Minor has come a long way since 1882, when its first store opened in Richmond. The company today has evolved from a family business to a Fortune 500 company that is the nation's leading distributor of national name-brand medical and surgical supplies. ∝ Throughout its history, Owens & Minor (O&M) has established a reputation for providing health care services with integrity, quality, and excellence. O&M strives to create solutions for customers and manufacturers while maximizing shareholder value. A major employer, O&M still considers its teammates to be part of the family.

From Cobblestone Streets to High Technology

In the products sold or the means by which they are distributed, the company today bears little resemblance to that shop which opened so long ago. Founded in 1882 by former competitors Otho O. Owens and George Gilmer Minor Jr., the Owens & Minor Drug Company first operated out of an iron-front building in downtown Richmond. In the beginning, a retail drug company occupied the front of the building,

Owens & Minor, led by Chairman and CEO G. Gilmer Minor III, has been a vital member of the Richmond business community since 1882.

while a wholesale operation operated out of the rear.

Instead of leather-bound ledgers and shipments by rail and wagon, business today depends on surging technology and rapid advances in medical care. Today, Owens & Minor serves hospitals, integrated health care systems, and group purchasing organizations across the United States, relying on expertise, technology, and a highly skilled work force. O&M involves a national network of facilities that employs approximately 2,800 professionals.

Still, the company's heart is the same. Its reputation for integrity, hard work, concern for community, caring about quality, loyalty to customers and suppliers, teamwork, and communication is deserved. While the form of the business is dramatically different, the values that support it are not.

The company's tradition of service in health-related fields has been carried forward through more than 100 years. From the beginning, the company was distinguished as a first-class operation, and through acquisitions and insightful changes, it has maintained this reputation.

Owens & Minor still considers family involvement to be a prominent characteristic of the business. G. Gilmer Minor III is chairman and CEO of the Richmond-based company, serving as the fourth G. Gilmer Minor to head the firm since its founding.

Progress and Growth

The company bought its first computer in 1954. That same year, it bought Bodeker Drug Company, the first in a series of acquisitions that triggered remarkable growth over two decades under the leadership of G. Gilmer Minor Jr. In 1971, in order to raise capital for continued growth, the company went public. Today, it is listed on the New York Stock Exchange.

The company serves 4,000 customers, including many of the top 15 hospitals in the United States, as ranked in the annual Best Hospitals Honor Roll published by *U.S. News & World Report*. The company works with 1,600 manufacturers to offer more than 170,000 products. In 2000, O&M's sales topped $3.5 billion. Also in 2000, the value of its common stock grew more than 98 percent.

In 1985, O&M won a multiyear contract with VHA (formerly Voluntary Hospitals of America), which set off another period of dynamic growth. In 1989, O&M passed another milestone with the purchase of National Healthcare. With this acquisition, the company established itself on the West Coast and became a national presence in the industry.

Through the generations, O&M has worked to develop superior expertise in supply chain management. It has invested in the latest technology, knowing that this investment would

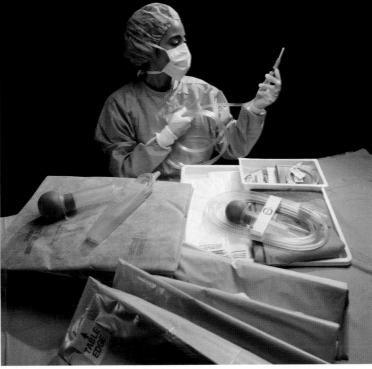

OWENS & MINOR IS A FORTUNE 500 COMPANY AND THE NATION'S LEADING DISTRIBUTOR OF NATIONAL NAME-BRAND MEDICAL AND SURGICAL SUPPLIES.

secure its industry dominance. O&M was rated 15th in an annual survey of the most innovative users of information technology in the country. That is the highest ranking of any health care company on the list.

And O&M has worked to maintain strong relationships with customers by offering the highest levels of customer service, recognizing that its success is based on its employees and their commitment to providing outstanding service to customers.

A Vital Part of the Richmond Community

"Owens & Minor is a vital and vibrant part of the Richmond community," Minor says. "Our volunteer team is active in many worthwhile causes. It's part of our mission to give back to the community. We take that very seriously."

Throughout this remarkable development, O&M has maintained its commitment to Richmond and to all the communities it serves. The company's employees across the country are encouraged to incorporate community service into their daily lives. Each year, teammates volunteer to work with charitable organizations such as United Way, Meals on Wheels, and the Make-a-Wish Foundation.

"We have grown along with the Richmond metropolitan area. Since 1882, Richmond has been our home.

The quality of life has allowed us to attract quality people to our organization," says Minor. "This is where our heart is."

The company's future is closely linked to the dynamic, growing industry it serves. Owens & Minor will be guided by an overall search for excellence measured by its customers' success. Taking lessons from its history, the company will continue to grow, relying on its strong foundation, its talented teammates, its technological sophistication, and its cultural reliance on mission, vision, and values.

The Jefferson Hotel

FROM THE FAUX MARBLE COLUMNS, THE GRAND STAIRCASE, THE magnificent stained glass, and the Carrara marble statue of Thomas Jefferson, to the refurbished guest rooms and suites, the charming, much-acclaimed Jefferson Hotel offers public and private spaces that are rich in detail and full of history. ❧ Few cities have so significant a place in American history as Richmond, and few hotels can claim so significant a place in a city's history as the Jefferson. Listed on the National Register of Historic Places, the hotel opened

in 1895 and has undergone renovations and expansions throughout its history. Within the last few years, the Jefferson underwent a $4 million enhancement program, which included the addition of a new courtyard entry with stone pavers, tiered fountain, and skylight porte cochere.

From the beginning, the Jefferson has been the place in Richmond for the grandest gatherings and celebrations. For executive meetings, conferences, fancy dress balls, wedding receptions, memorable banquets, and other occasions, the Jefferson offers 18 distinct meeting rooms that provide privacy, flexibility, beauty, and elegance. Its Grand Ballroom, with gold-detailed ceiling and magnificent crystal chandelier, and the beautiful Empire Room provide perfect settings for larger, more formal functions.

The hotel contains 260 guestrooms and suites in more than 50 styles. All include high ceilings, tall windows, custom-designed furnishings, and refined artwork. For the Jefferson's demanding clientele, the hotel provides sophisticated security, a fleet of town cars, tour services, shopping,

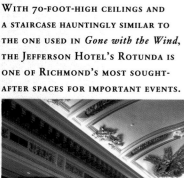

and a health club with indoor swimming pool.

For business travelers, the hotel has set up as many as 200 secured phone lines, drop-link satellite hookups, courier service, and a full range of audiovisual facilities, including recording and production services.

The Jefferson has played host to nine presidents, the prestigious Fortune 500 Forum, and dozens of cotillions, shareholders' meetings, and other noteworthy events. From Elvis to Sinatra, Charlie Chaplin to Warren Beatty, F. Scott Fitzgerald to William Styron, luminaries who come to Richmond stay at the Jefferson.

The Place to Be

The Jefferson is located on historic Franklin Street, one of the city's most elegant addresses, just blocks from the Virginia capitol—designed by Thomas Jefferson—as well as museums, business centers, and other points of interest. Its staff, from the parking valets to the concierge, are genuinely welcoming to every guest.

Despite the comfort the Jefferson's rooms provide, most guests enjoy relaxing beneath the towering Rotunda, where first-class beverage service is offered each evening at the foot of the sweeping Grand Staircase. Legend

BUILT IN 1895, THE JEFFERSON HOTEL RECENTLY COMPLETED A $4 MILLION RENOVATION, WHICH INCLUDES THE ADDITION OF A GRAND NEW ENTRANCE AND ELEGANT PORTE COCHERE, A STUNNING INDOOR SWIMMING POOL AND A GLASS CONSERVATORY TO THE HOTEL'S AAA FIVE-DIAMOND RESTAURANT, LEMAIRE.

WITH 70-FOOT-HIGH CEILINGS AND A STAIRCASE HAUNTINGLY SIMILAR TO THE ONE USED IN *Gone with the Wind*, THE JEFFERSON HOTEL'S ROTUNDA IS ONE OF RICHMOND'S MOST SOUGHT-AFTER SPACES FOR IMPORTANT EVENTS.

has it the staircase was used in *Gone with the Wind*, and though this is indeed pure legend, Richmonders love to tell the tale, and visitors are inclined to believe. Roving newsman Charles Kuralt once described the Rotunda as "arguably the most beautiful [public room] of any hotel in the country."

When he came from Philadelphia to Richmond to manage the Jefferson, Joseph Longo says he was shocked to find the hotel's public rooms and restaurants bustling on Christmas Eve, traditionally one of the slowest nights of the year in the hotel business. "People were drinking champagne, exchanging gifts under the tree," he says. "That really tells you something about the hotel and how the city feels about it."

World-Class Dining

Named for Thomas Jefferson's maître d', Lemaire consists of seven separate dining rooms, including the Library, whose shelves contain original leather-bound volumes dating to 1895, the year the hotel opened. With an executive chef trained at the prestigious Culinary Institute of America, Lemaire extends a sumptuous menu that combines European influences with Southern tradition. To meet growing demand, the restaurant recently opened a glass-enclosed, Victorian-style conservatory to offer elegant dining with a view of historic Franklin Street.

The Jefferson also offers casual dining at TJ's Restaurant and Lounge, where guests enjoy lunch, dinner, and late-night fare in a relaxed atmosphere overlooking the Rotunda. From classic chicken salad to crab

cakes to Monticello oyster chowder, TJ's provides a full menu for the informal business lunch or a break from shopping.

Both the hotel and Lemaire have earned the prestigious AAA five-diamond rating for several years. To second that recognition, the Jefferson Hotel is also a Mobil Five-Star Award winner, making it one of only 17 in North America to hold both coveted ratings.

Richmond's Own

According to Longo, the two secrets to the Jefferson's success are the commitment of its owners and the outstanding staff. The owners, Richmond businessmen who purchased the hotel in 1991, are independent of any chain. They know what the hotel means to the city and are willing to invest the time and money necessary to provide

"history, service, and a wonderful hotel, all at a very reasonable rate," Longo says. "Every time we've needed to improve something, they've stepped up. They are committed to making this one of the world's finest hotels."

This investment has created at the Jefferson "a great environment for employees," says Longo. "Ownership demands that every guest have a great experience here, and we've been able to put the right people in the right places to do that. The staff here is outstanding."

Still, the hotel's ownership and management cannot afford to rest. The Mobil Five-Star and AAA five-diamond ratings are the standard they intend to meet, and the bar is being raised every year. "We have to improve ourselves constantly," Longo says. "We want, and expect, every guest to have a perfect experience."

CLOCKWISE FROM TOP LEFT: THE JEFFERSON HOTEL HAS 260 LUXURIOUS GUEST ROOMS AND SUITES THAT FEATURE 57 DELIGHTFULLY DIFFERENT STYLES, ALL WITH UNUSUALLY HIGH CEILINGS, TALL WINDOWS, AND CUSTOM-DESIGNED UPHOLSTERED FURNISHINGS.

TO CREATE A NEW DINING EXPERIENCE FOR ITS GUESTS, THE JEFFERSON HOTEL RECENTLY ADDED AN ORNATE, GLASS-ENCLOSED, VICTORIAN-STYLE CONSERVATORY TO ITS AAA FIVE-DIAMOND RESTAURANT, LEMAIRE.

THE INDOOR SWIMMING POOL, LOCATED ON THE JEFFERSON'S FIRST FLOOR, ALLOWS GUESTS TO BATHE BENEATH SUN- OR STARLIT SKYLIGHTS.

PricewaterhouseCoopers LLP

PRICEWATERHOUSECOOPERS LLP (PwC), ONE OF THE WORLD'S largest professional services organizations, is an active contributor to the Richmond area's corporate and cultural well-being. Created by the merger in 1998 of two businesses—Price Waterhouse and Coopers & Lybrand—whose roots go back to London and the 1850s, the firm today helps a variety of clients solve complex business problems, while it measurably

enhances the clients' ability to build value, manage risks, and improve performance.

Simply stated, PwC's job is channeling knowledge and value through six lines of service and 22 industries. The company "is there to serve you wherever you are" by taking its global web of expertise and putting it to use locally. Today, Richmond is one of PwC's major business centers.

Serving the Region's Foremost Businesses

Currently, PwC employs more than 160,000 partners and staff in 150 countries. More than 80 people work in the company's Richmond office, most of them in assurance/business advisory services or with tax and legal services. The firm is housed in a scenic and practical location in the prestigious Riverfront Towers high-rise office complex between the James River and the city's busy financial district.

PwC's clients are among the region's foremost businesses, including Albemarle Corporation; Amurcon Corporation of Virginia; Bear Island Paper Company; Chesapeake Corporation; Christian Children's Fund; Colonnade Capital; Ethyl Corporation; Ferguson Enterprises; Jefferson Capital; Noland Company; Quad-C, Inc.; S&K Famous Brands; Sabot

Publishing; Southern States Cooperative; and Stanley Furniture Company.

These businesses and others take advantage of PwC's six lines of service, which have been developed over the years to reflect the demands of today's intensely competitive, technology-reliant global marketplace. The company is among the world's leaders in each discipline that it has entered, and the firm has the capacity to deploy skilled, highly qualified professionals when and where needed.

The industries PwC serves fall into three clusters: consumer and industrial products, energy, mining, and service industries; technology, information, communication, and entertainment; and financial services. The company's

six lines of service include its audit, assurance, and business advisory group, which helps organizations with financial control, regulatory reporting, shareholder value, and technology issues.

Global human resources and insurance management are included in PwC's services, as is management consulting in areas such as strategic change management, process improvement, and technology solutions. Deals with business process outsourcing, which includes the areas of finance and accounting, internal auditing, tax compliance, applications processes, procurement, and real estate services, are available through the company as well.

STAFF MEMBERS IN THE RICHMOND OFFICE OF PRICEWATERHOUSECOOPERS LLP RELY ON A GLOBAL WEB OF EXPERTISE TO PROVIDE A RANGE OF PROFESSIONAL SERVICES TO LOCAL BUSINESSES.

The company's global tax service includes formulating effective strategies for optimizing taxes, implementing innovative tax planning, and helping businesses to effectively maintain compliance with varied tax requirements. PwC's financial advisory service includes providing comprehensive financial, economic, and strategic advice to companies with complex business problems and disputes.

Providing Useful Information to Leaders and Investors

The company makes available useful, provocative, and relevant materials of worldwide scope, written by some of the firm's and the world's most accredited thinkers and doers. PwC is a leader in using new technology to gather and disseminate this information.

PwC's highly regarded on-line business magazine includes an executive digest that covers issues, events, and new ideas that will help prepare corporate leaders for the challenges ahead. Whether they are keeping an eye on China, Latin America, Russia, or other emerging centers, or examining financial instruments, derivatives exchanges, or organizational change, PwC's contributors are ahead of the curve.

PwC can also link businesses with on-line sources of solutions, including a comprehensive library of authoritative financial reporting and assurance literature. Its tax news network is a vital source of focused information for the tax professional.

The company offers quarterly surveys of more than 1,000 CEOs, CFOs, and managing directors of leading U.S. companies. These surveys pro-

vide trend indicators and industry directions for fast-growth and technology firms.

PwC offers on-line products, as well, that assist financial institutions in assessing their own progress in developing, marketing, and leveraging electronic channels to help them better serve customers and reduce costs.

More than 40 researchers, software developers, and technology analysts from the PwC's Technology Center can provide analysis and evaluation of emerging information technologies via the firm's on-line connections.

The company's most frequently requested publications include its practical, authoritative *Doing Business* guides; *Guide for Businessmen and Investors* series; and technology forecasts.

Maintaining an Active Role in the Community

Beyond its contributions to the region's corporate culture and business needs, PwC's employees can be found giving hours of their time to local boards and

community service groups. These include the Boys and Girls Club of Metro Richmond, Big Brothers/Big Sisters, Greater Richmond Chamber of Commerce, Richmond Symphony, Mathematics and Science Center Foundation, READ Center, Theatre IV, TheatreVirginia, Salvation Army, Virginia One to One, Junior Achievement, Westminster Canterbury, and World Affairs Council.

While PwC Richmond has one employee who serves on the board of the National Association of Black Accountants, others are members of organizations such as the Virginia Museum of Fine Arts, Hand Workshop Art Center, Juvenile Diabetes Foundation, American Diabetes Foundation, Virginia Chapter Future Business Leaders of America, and Western Henrico Rotary Club.

Through these community activities and the company's dynamic role in the corporate sector, PricewaterhouseCoopers LLC will play a leading role in the development of central Virginia well into the future.

MORE THAN 80 PEOPLE WORK IN PwC's RICHMOND OFFICES, MOST OF THEM IN ASSURANCE/BUSINESS ADVISORY SERVICES OR WITH TAX AND LEGAL SERVICES.

*M*ANY YEARS OF RICHMOND'S HISTORY, ITS MARRIAGE proposals, significant promotions, and special occasions have been celebrated by the passing of gifts that are enclosed in Schwarzschild Jewelers' blue boxes. In a city where tradition is so deeply valued, no other tradition sets hearts aflutter more readily than giving gifts from this fine jewelry store. ❧ It was 1897 when 18-year-old William Harry (W.H.)

Schwarzschild, the son of a European immigrant, founded the Old Dominion Watch Company in Richmond. An industrious young man, Schwarzschild thought there was a market for good watches in this booming railroad and industry town. He soon discovered that his customers, many of whom were affluent, also wanted fobs, chains, and pins. So Schwarzschild's business expanded to accommodate them.

In 1902, he was joined by his brother Gustavus, and the business changed its name to Schwarzschild Brothers. Over time, younger brothers Sollie and Henry would join. All were active throughout their lifetimes in Richmond's social and business circles, as well as in significant real estate developments. W.H. founded the Central National Bank and built its headquarters tower, a Richmond architectural landmark, on Broad Street near Schwarzschild's downtown store. He also was a founder of the Retail Merchants Association and served as president of the Richmond Chamber of Commerce.

Committed to Quality and Service
Today, like Tiffany in New York and Neiman-Marcus in Dallas, the Schwarzschild name is synonymous with luxury in Richmond. "With the legacy we have established for full service and high quality, Schwarzschild has truly become Richmond's jeweler," says Wendy Kreuter, great-great-granddaughter of the founder. While the business invites a broad range of clients inside its doors, Schwarzschild carries such highly prized brands as Mikimoto pearls, Cartier and Breitling watches, and Lazare diamonds.

In an era of chain jewelry stores, Schwarzschild is clearly distinguished by its legacy and by its commitment to quality. It provides its customers with the full range of services—from its popular bridal registry to a complete repair shop. Schwarzschild also can give appraisals, and maintains a jewelry designer on staff.

The company continues to operate from the flagship store at Broad and Second Streets, a location that has prospered through decades when other retailers pulled out of Richmond's historic retail core. Now, as that grand old part of the city undergoes a revitalization, Schwarzschild is in place, ready to serve new neighbors and long-time customers downtown. The company also operates stores in Regency Square Mall in Richmond's West End, and in Carytown, one of the region's most unique shopping centers.

Growing Toward Richmond's Future
The Schwarzschild family maintains connections to the business. Tracy Schwarzschild, a local lawyer, is on the company's board. And Wendy Kreuter works as a buyer and runs the company's human resources division. "It's good to maintain those ties," Kreuter says. "We want to keep firmly connected to our roots. That's who we are."

Kreuter says that as Richmond grows, Schwarzschild Jewelers is looking seriously at developing new locations in the metro area. Whatever decisions the company makes to expand, Richmonders know that inside Schwarzschild's stores, as in its blue boxes, they will find something that will be a special treasure for years to come.

THE SCHWARZSCHILD FLAGSHIP STORE AT BROAD AND SECOND STREETS, SHOWN HERE EARLY IN THE LAST CENTURY, WAS OPENED IN 1903 (TOP).

SCHWARZSCHILD HAS ALWAYS BEEN KNOWN FOR EXCEPTIONAL DIAMONDS AND GEMS. SHOWN HERE ARE A SELECTION OF FANCY-SHAPE DIAMOND RINGS FROM THE SCHWARZSCHILD COLLECTION (BOTTOM).

DYNAMIC AND INNOVATIVE ARE TWO TERMS THAT CHARACTER-
ize a Richmond-based law firm with both a long-standing presence in the area and a reputation for excellence. Hunton & Williams, founded in 1901, has become a major player in
the international marketplace. With more than 750 lawyers in 15 offices in the United States
and overseas, Hunton & Williams responds to the increasingly complex demands of

its clients. At the same time, the firm sustains the sense of camaraderie, intellectual adventure, and commitment to higher purpose that has fueled the practice from its beginning.

Leading Legal Minds

The backgrounds and fields of experience of Hunton & Williams' lawyers are diverse: They come from almost every state and from several countries, having graduated from 65 different law schools. This breadth of perspective enables the firm to provide the highest-quality legal services in all areas of the law and across cultures.

Practicing at the firm today are a former U.S. ambassador, a former governor and attorney general of Virginia, the first African-American lawyer to serve as a justice of the Virginia Supreme Court, and a distinguished former federal judge of national renown. Former partners at the firm have gone on to service on the U.S. Supreme Court and the U.S. District Courts, in the U.S. Senate, and as the dean of a major law school.

Hunton & Williams' attorneys operate in a culture in which they are expected to work hard in the best interests of clients, of society, and of the law. This combination of skilled professionals working together has earned Hunton & Williams a ranking among the top 50 law firms in the world.

Recognized as experts in many areas, Hunton & Williams' lawyers provide expertise to clients, regardless of size or location. International corporations, foreign and domestic governments, Internet service providers, financial institutions, venture capitalists, and emerging businesses comprise the firm's varied client list.

Capital markets, information technologies, project finance, litigation, environmental, energy and telecommunications, and intellectual property are among the firm's more than 50 distinct practice areas. Hunton & Williams is also at the forefront in

new and rapidly evolving fields such as biotechnology, privacy, hazardous wastes, European competition, and immigration.

Community Contribution

Across the Richmond region, throughout Virginia, and around the United States, Hunton & Williams' lawyers are active in pro bono work and in charitable, religious, and educational organizations. They serve as board members for colleges and universities, museums, and other cultural entities, and are members of conservation, restoration, and community action groups.

Every year since the American Bar Association issued its pro bono challenge, setting as its standard a commitment of 3 percent of gross billable hours for services to the poor, Hunton & Williams has exceeded that goal. Though 1999 was the busiest year in the firm's history, Hunton & Williams set a record for the amount of time, number of lawyers, and number of matters handled for charitable and civic organizations. In recognition of this achievement, the American Bar Association gave Hunton & Williams its *Pro Bono Publico* Award.

For nearly a century, Hunton & Williams has provided superior legal services, doing so always with a commitment to its clients, a respect to society, and a thorough understanding of the law. Today, with hundreds of lawyers and hundreds more employees living, working, and contributing to life in the area, Hunton & Williams has established itself as one of the premier law firms in the world, as well as a valuable asset to the Richmond community.

GORDON RAINEY (LEFT) IS HUNTON & WILLIAMS' EXECUTIVE COMMITTEE CHAIRMAN, AND THURSTON MOORE (RIGHT) IS MANAGING PARTNER.

WITH HUNDREDS OF LAWYERS AND HUNDREDS MORE EMPLOYEES LIVING, WORKING, AND CONTRIBUTING TO LIFE IN THE AREA, HUNTON & WILLIAMS HAS ESTABLISHED ITSELF AS ONE OF THE PREMIER LAW FIRMS IN THE WORLD, AS WELL AS A VALUABLE ASSET TO THE RICHMOND COMMUNITY.

1909 *Dominion*

1911 *St. Christopher's School*

1914 *Federal Reserve Bank of Richmond*

1915 *Collegiate School*

1919 *Brown Distributing Company*

1937 *Ukrop's Super Markets, Inc.*

1948 *WTVR-TV*

1956 *WWBT/NBC12*

1957 *Cushing Manufacturing Co.*

1957 *David R. McGeorge Car Co., Inc.*

1958 *Virginia Sprinkler Company, Inc.*

WITH ROOTS THAT CAN BE TRACED BACK TO THE 18TH CENTURY and a modern history at the core of Virginia's new economy, Dominion Virginia Power has established itself as a leader in the emerging competitive energy marketplace. Experienced, reliable, innovative, aggressive–Richmond-based Dominion has assets exceeding $28 billion and is one of the nation's largest integrated energy companies. In the past decade, the company has spent hundreds of millions of dollars on improvements to customer services and operations.

Growth with the Region

While the Virginia Railway & Power Company was incorporated in 1909, in a sense, the company's corporate roots go back to the 1788 founding of the Appomattox Trustees, a public service company formed to enhance navigation on the Appomattox River. Virginia Railway, founded by Frank Northrup, provided electric trolley service in Richmond and central Virginia. Incidentally, the company sold excess electricity not needed for trolleys to homes and businesses along its route.

In 1925, the firm changed its name to Virginia Electric & Power Company and became known to customers as Vepco. In the next three-quarters of a century, the company saw dramatic growth as it acquired smaller utilities and expanded operations. Vepco also became an investor-owned utility.

In 1984, the firm formed a holding company, Dominion Resources Inc., and changed its name from Vepco to Virginia Power. In 1999, under the leadership of Thomas E. Capps, president and chairman, Dominion Resources merged with Consolidated Natural Gas to become one of the nation's

WITH ROOTS THAT CAN BE TRACED BACK TO THE 18TH CENTURY AND A MODERN HISTORY AT THE CORE OF VIRGINIA'S NEW ECONOMY, DOMINION VIRGINIA POWER HAS ESTABLISHED ITSELF AS A LEADER IN THE EMERGING COMPETITIVE ENERGY MARKETPLACE.

largest integrated energy companies.

In 2000, Dominion Resources announced it would operate as Dominion. Today, Dominion is a completely integrated gas and electric company that has become a leader in the emerging competitive energy marketplace.

Dominion sells electricity and natural gas to more than 4 million customers in five states. The company also sells a variety of energy-related and telecommunications services in the same area, as well as maintains a vast gas pipeline system that reaches into the northeastern United States.

Dominion operates out of a number of major offices in Richmond, including its corporate headquarters– a handsome brick complex on the banks of the James River. A 20-story tower, One James River Plaza holds many of the company's administrative functions, and a modern complex at Innsbrook in western Henrico County houses the firm's extensive technical operations.

Public Service and a Promising Future

Dominion and its predecessors have always taken their role as a public service company seriously. Toward that end, Dominion formed a volunteer program that has twice won White House recognition and has drawn praise from state and local leaders.

The company also created EnergyShare, a program to help those in need keep their homes warm on cold winter days. Through EnergyShare, the company has distributed millions of dollars to those with no place else to turn.

"Dominion and its corporate ancestors have been part of the Virginia landscape for almost a century," says Capps. "We're proud of our Virginia roots and the contributions we've made to the Commonwealth's growth. We intend to build on this long tradition of service and help Virginia achieve even greater prosperity in the future."

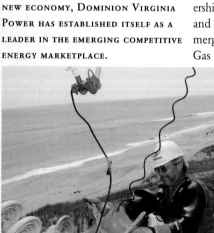

ᖴOUNDED IN 1915, COLLEGIATE SCHOOL OFFERS ITS SOME 1,500 students small classes and close contact with its more than 180 faculty members, who inspire young people to achieve both academically and personally. From kindergarten onward, Collegiate prepares students to meet the high standards of its college preparatory program and to go on to be positive, contributing members of the community. ᘛ The

school offers students numerous opportunities to excel and develop in the classroom and in extracurricular activities. Students are taught the value of ethics, honor, and respect, as the honor code is a valued part of the school's legacy. Sportsmanship is emphasized on the court and field.

Education Today for Tomorrow

Collegiate School's 55-acre campus in Richmond's residential western Henrico County includes expansive facilities where students can explore their interests in academics, athletics, technology, and the arts. On campus, there are athletic fields, a track, four gyms, and eight tennis courts, in addition to 12 more practice fields on 155 acres just 10 minutes from the school. The acclaimed Hershey Center for the Arts features the 620-seat Oates Theater, considered one of the finest theaters in Richmond, as well as art, music, and drama studios and a photography darkroom.

Collegiate has assumed a leading role in educating young people in the application of technology. With more than 500 computers in classrooms and labs, as well as a campuswide network that provides in-house E-mail and a high-speed Internet connection, students and faculty have easy access to each other and the world. The new Lower School Library/Technology Center and the Middle and Upper School science buildings are all fully wired to maximize potential for research and experimentation.

Knowledge for All Ages

Collegiate School includes three divisions: the Lower School, kindergarten through fourth grade; the Middle School, grades five through eight; and the Upper School, grades nine through 12. Core educational concepts are introduced to Lower School students. From the beginning, students are exposed to technology, foreign languages, and basic values.

Community service is part of the school experience as well.

The Middle School experience is rigorous, with flexibility to allow students to explore their interests and talents. Though Collegiate is a coeducational school, at this level boys and girls take academic classes separately. Students in this challenging period of life interact with a faculty adviser daily, as part of a nationally recognized advisory program. In seventh and eighth grades, Collegiate also offers a no-cut athletic program for all students interested in sports. Community service and the school's honor code become increasingly important at this level.

Competitive sports, music and drama, clubs, travel, and study abroad all are available to students in Collegiate's Upper School. The goal is for each individual to maximize his or her academic potential. As students mature, they are given increasing opportunities and challenges to develop their intellect and independence.

A tribute to the school's dedication to the futures of its students is Collegiate's 100 percent rate of graduates attending a four-year college or university, including among their choices the nation's most prestigious institutions. With a focus on academic and personal achievement and a list of noted alumni, Collegiate School will continue its educational legacy for years to come.

COLLEGIATE SCHOOL'S 55-ACRE CAMPUS IN RICHMOND'S RESIDENTIAL WESTERN HENRICO COUNTY INCLUDES EXPANSIVE FACILITIES WHERE STUDENTS CAN EXPLORE THEIR INTERESTS IN ACADEMICS, ATHLETICS, TECHNOLOGY, AND THE ARTS.

For some 90 years, St. Christopher's School has provided an exceptional environment for the education and development of boys from throughout the Greater Richmond area. Today, with the leadership of a youthful headmaster and an outstanding and caring faculty, St. Christopher's is building upon its traditional strengths and continuing its role as an energetic, vibrant, innovative center that serves the broader Richmond community. Founded by Dr. Churchill Gibson Chamberlayne in 1911, the Chamberlayne School became part of a system of church schools of the Episcopal Diocese of Virginia in June of 1920. It was then that the name was changed to St. Christopher's School.

Tradition and Innovation

Situated on a 58-acre campus in Richmond's Westhampton neighborhood, St. Christopher's enrolls approximately 900 boys from junior kindergarten through grade 12. The school's campus is a comfortable gathering of red brick buildings, shaded walkways, and spacious athletic fields. Recent additions, including a $3.5 million Lower School addition and a $4 million science center, have dramatically improved the school's facilities.

Headmaster Charley Stillwell says the school—located in Richmond, but close to major population centers in surrounding counties—is well positioned geographically to play an expanded role in the Richmond region. "We are a school where boys from all over can come together to work on projects, to play, and to grow together," Stillwell says. "Here, we help build bonds of trust and friendship that cross divisions in our community, and include a diverse population. We can and do make a difference."

Since his 1998 arrival on campus,

Stillwell says he's discovered a school with boundless energy and enthusiasm, one that has launched new initiatives aimed at better serving its students and the community. "I knew St. Christopher's had great traditional strength, but underneath that there is also energy and excitement," says Stillwell. "What we're doing now is building on this marriage of tradition and innovation."

St. Christopher's offers a variety of programs that are open to the Greater Richmond community. The new science center is utilized not only by St. Christopher's students and faculty, but also by area teachers who come to the center for continuing education and enrichment programs. During the school year, the school's renowned concert series brings to campus professional musicians whose performances are free and open to the public. In the summer, the school hosts institutes in math and science, creative writing, and leadership and public service.

The St. Christopher's Experience

St. Christopher's is widely recognized for its focus on developing the whole boy. As it seeks to accomplish this, the school offers a strong core liberal arts program augmented with a wide array of electives in foreign languages, computer science, and the fine arts. The school is proud of its rigorous academic program, honor system, participation in athletics and the arts, and commitment to community service.

At St. Christopher's, chapel brings the school community together to worship, celebrate achievements, and listen to outstanding speakers. Alumni have strong ties to the school, and come back often to share their time and talents. "In addition to our outstanding faculty, there are some incredible adults, both alumni and parents, who work with our boys," says headmaster Charley Stillwell.

Community service is an important part of the St. Christopher's experience as well. Students work as both individuals and groups to help others in the community. Some tutor children in reading and math, while others volunteer their talents in improving the environment or working with senior citizens.

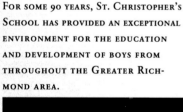

FOR SOME 90 YEARS, ST. CHRISTOPHER'S SCHOOL HAS PROVIDED AN EXCEPTIONAL ENVIRONMENT FOR THE EDUCATION AND DEVELOPMENT OF BOYS FROM THROUGHOUT THE GREATER RICHMOND AREA.

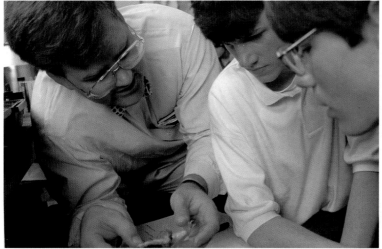

St. Christopher's students are required to participate in athletics, which include 13 varsity sports, as well as a year-round outward-bound program of canoeing and rock climbing. They enjoy indoor track and tennis courts, gyms for basketball and wrestling, a track complex, and weight training and fitness rooms. The focus of the athletic program is on developing lifelong habits of exercise, fitness, and nutrition.

Academic Opportunities

With its college preparatory orientation, St. Christopher's offers extensive counseling services and a wide range of advanced placement courses. St. Christopher's offers more than $1 million in financial assistance in a variety of forms each year to help deserving students who could not otherwise afford to attend the school. Aid is awarded on the basis of need. Approximately 45 college recruiters visit the campus each year, and, not surprisingly, St. Christopher's gradu-

ates earn admission to some of the finest colleges and universities in the region and the nation.

Although St. Christopher's is a school for boys, it has a cooperative partnership with nearby sister school St. Catherine's, a highly rated private school for girls. Special activities are shared at every grade level, while each school maintains separate academic classrooms in the Lower and Middle schools.

In the Upper School, students can take classes on either campus, providing them with an excellent opportunity in which boys and girls interact within the classroom and other programs, yet giving them the feel of a smaller school with more personal attention from the individual school faculties. This cooperative relationship also broadens the number of courses available to students on both campuses. Students can take classes with teachers from both faculties, and are able to enjoy a wealth of facilities. The schools' partnership also doubles

the leadership opportunities for students.

"St. Christopher's is a place that has a wonderful academic program, yet the academics here are just a starting point," Stillwell says. "What we are building is an exceptional environment for developing the whole boy. The young men who come out of here are going to be leaders in their communities. They are going to have an array of abilities that will enable them to make a difference. They are going to be people of character who see working hard and contributing to their communities as a way of life."

St. Christopher's is widely recognized for its focus on developing the whole boy. As it seeks to accomplish this, the school offers a strong core liberal arts program augmented with a wide array of electives in foreign languages, computer science, and the fine arts.

St. Christopher's graduates earn admission to some of the finest colleges and universities in the region and the nation.

THE FEDERAL RESERVE BANK OF RICHMOND OCCUPIES A prominent spot in Richmond's skyline. Equally prominent is the Richmond Fed's role in ensuring the financial stability of the nation. The Federal Reserve Act, signed by President Woodrow Wilson in 1913, created a system to provide the nation with a safer, more efficient, and more stable monetary and financial system. The system is composed

of a central board of governors in Washington, D.C., and 12 reserve banks located in major cities across the nation. Richmond, the smallest of the 12 cities, was chosen largely because of the work of Carter Glass, a Virginia congressman who was an adviser to Wilson and chairman of the House Committee on Banking and Finance.

The Federal Reserve Bank of Richmond opened its doors in 1914, bolstering the city's prominence as a regional financial center. From rented space, the bank's 20 employees began serving commercial banks in the Fifth Federal Reserve District, which includes the District of Columbia, Maryland, North Carolina, South Carolina, Virginia, and most of West Virginia. Today, the Fifth District is home to banking

institutions that control more than 19 percent of the country's commercial banking assets, the second-largest concentration of such assets in the nation. As the district's headquarters, the Richmond Fed employs more than 1,700 people, making it one of the city's largest employers.

To Foster Stability

According to J. Alfred Broaddus Jr., a Richmond native and the Richmond Fed's president, "The bank brings a great many jobs to the area, many of them high-level professional jobs. Beyond this, the Richmond community can be proud that this hometown Fed unit is conducting research and making recommendations that contribute directly to national monetary and banking policies."

The Federal Reserve promotes a healthy economy and a stable financial system. The Richmond Fed contributes to this role by conducting research on macroeconomics, banking, and the payments system, and, most directly, by contributing to the evaluation and formation of monetary policy. The Richmond Fed president serves as a voting member on the Federal Open Market Committee (FOMC) on a rotating basis. The FOMC's decisions affect the cost and availability of money and credit, impacting businesses and consumers alike.

Because of this impact, visitors to the Richmond Fed may ask employees to speculate about interest rates. The most frequent question, however, involves how many billions of dollars are stored underground.

THE FEDERAL RESERVE BANK OF RICHMOND HOLDS A PROMINENT PLACE IN RICHMOND'S DOWNTOWN SKYLINE.

▼ GEEP SCHURMAN, FEDERAL RESERVE BANK OF RICHMOND

Most people know the regional Fed offices put into circulation the money the Treasury prints or mints. They are also usually aware that the Fed removes damaged, counterfeit, and worn-out currency from circulation. Less well known, but even more impressive, is the bank's role in assuring the electronic transfer of $145 billion daily for financial institutions in the Fifth District.

The responsibility for the efficiency and effectiveness of the U.S. payments system rests squarely with the Federal Reserve. As the "banker's bank," the Fed provides services to financial institutions. Every day, reserve banks process hundreds of billions of dollars through currency, check, and electronic payment services. In addition to services provided to financial institutions, reserve banks serve as banks for the U.S. government by maintaining accounts and providing services for the Treasury.

Through its regional banks, the Fed also supervises and regulates the increasingly complex operations of commercial banks and other depository institutions. Richmond's examiners work with other federal and state entities to promote safety and soundness in the operation of financial institutions, stability in the financial markets, and fair and equitable treatment of consumers in their financial transactions.

Rooted in Richmond

With the growth of the Fifth District's economy, the Richmond Fed's responsibilities and its subsequent need for space have grown. In 1978, after 60 years and several locations, the Federal Reserve Bank of Richmond moved into its $60 million headquarters on East Byrd Street. This 26-story tower stands at the front of Richmond's skyline as seen by travelers coming north into the city. Designed by Minoru Yamasaki and Associates, the downtown building contains almost one million square feet of space, 45 percent of which is below ground.

This move to an eight-acre site located on the James River placed the Richmond Fed as a leader in the redevelopment of the historic Main-to-the-James district. It opened a two-block pedestrian walkway along the Haxall Canal in 1991, preceding the current revitalization of Richmond's downtown waterfront.

The bank's leaders and workers have historically taken prominent roles in the Richmond community. And the bank's physical presence on the downtown waterfront has provided symbolic and real impetus for growth and development.

Because the bank relies on a base of increasingly sophisticated professionals, it is a valuable resource in a city of any size, bringing educated and experienced people to town. In a smaller city, by Federal Reserve standards, the bank's impact is even greater. Its employees—including bank examiners, economists, computer engineers, technicians, accountants, and service workers—provide leadership and service to a variety of community organizations. The bank also works with the area's colleges and universities to recruit and develop a strong workforce for the future.

Contributing to tomorrow's workforce development, the Federal Reserve Bank of Richmond seeks to provide information and educational resources that promote an understanding of the economy and the forces that shape it.

VALENTINE MUSEUM, RICHMOND, VIRGINIA

GEEP SCHURMAN, FEDERAL RESERVE BANK OF RICHMOND

THE RICHMOND FED OPENED ITS DOORS IN 1914 ON EAST MAIN STREET. IT MOVED TO ITS THIRD AND CURRENT LOCATION AT 7TH AND BYRD STREETS IN 1978 (TOP).

A CASH SERVICES EMPLOYEE LOADS A HIGH-SPEED CURRENCY SORTER. THESE SORTERS CAN COUNT, SORT, OR DESTROY AN AVERAGE OF 80,000 NOTES PER HOUR. THE RICHMOND FED PROCESSES CHECKS, CARRIES OUT WIRE-TRANSFER TRANSACTIONS, AND DISTRIBUTES COIN AND CURRENCY TO DEPOSITORY INSTITUTIONS THROUGHOUT THE FIFTH FEDERAL RESERVE DISTRICT (BOTTOM LEFT).

THE CANNONBALL SAFE IS HOUSED IN THE BANK'S MONEY MUSEUM. MUSEUM EXHIBITS TELL THE STORY OF MONEY IN COLONIAL AMERICA AND THE UNITED STATES, AND DISPLAY PRIMITIVE MONIES AND MEDIEVAL AND ANCIENT COINS. THE MUSEUM IS SELF-GUIDED AND OPEN TO THE PUBLIC. THE BANK ALSO OFFERS GUIDED TOURS OF ITS FACILITIES (BOTTOM RIGHT).

KEN ANDERSON, FEDERAL RESERVE BANK OF RICHMOND

Brown Distributing Company

In 1919, BROTHERS ABRAHAM AND ISADORE BROWN FORMED A soda-bottling business with a plant located on Brook Road, where they produced a cherry-flavored soft drink. In 1926, the Brown brothers acquired the rights to Try-Me beverages and undertook the first of many expansions. With that step, the company moved to larger quarters on West Main Street. Today, the Brown brothers' business serves some 2,000

retailers throughout central Virginia as it maintains an active role in community events, charities, and various service organizations. The company employs more than 150 people and operates a fleet of 125 vehicles in the greater Richmond area.

Prohibition Ends;
Anheuser-Busch Begins

The end of Prohibition in 1933 launched the Browns into the beer distribution business, the company's source of success. Beginning in 1933, the company added Wolf Beer, which was brewed in Philadelphia, and Gunter's Beer, which was brewed in Baltimore,

to its soft drink portfolio. The Browns' delivery trucks carried both soft drinks and malt beverages to retailers in Richmond, Petersburg, and throughout the surrounding area. In 1935, Pepsi Co. appointed the brothers to be its bottler for the Richmond-Petersburg area. By then, the Try-Me Beverage Company, as it was still known, had a fleet of six trucks and 10 employees.

The next step in the company's growth came in 1936, when Anheuser-Busch Inc. of St. Louis approached some existing business owners in the Commonwealth, including Abraham and Isadore Brown, and asked them to franchise its Budweiser and Michelob draft beers.

In 1938, the company changed its name from Try-Me to Pepsi Cola Bottling Company of Richmond. By this time, it occupied two bottling facilities and warehouses. In 1947, the brothers ended their partnership. In 1951, Abraham and his son Jacob formed Brown Distributing Company. By 1956, the company had completely outgrown the West Main Street space and moved into a new location on Rhoadmiller Road.

The 1960s saw the introduction of a new Anheuser-Busch product, Busch beer. In 1969, Brown sold its Pepsi

Cola operation. A few years later, Jacob's son, Larry Brown, joined the business.

A Part of the Richmond Family

In 1971, Brown Distributing moved again, this time to the location where it operates today, on Byrdhill Road. In the 1970s, its fleet had grown to 16 trucks. In 1977, Anheuser-Busch's new Natural Light beer was added to the company portfolio, and in 1978, Michelob Light joined the product line. Bud Light was introduced in 1982, and that same year, the company acquired the distribution rights to the popular import Heineken.

The Browns further expanded their business in 1984, acquiring another distribution operation in West Palm Beach, Florida. Two years later, they celebrated 50 years of distributing Anheuser-Busch products.

Larry Brown continues to run the company, and the children continue to be involved. Brown Distributing is a presence at almost every community event in the area. Brown and his wife, Betty, are active in children's charities, employee assistance programs, and alcohol abuse prevention programs. This family-owned and -operated business continues to play an active role in the Greater Richmond area.

CLOCKWISE FROM TOP:
LARRY BROWN AND HIS WIFE, BETTY, ARE ACTIVE IN CHILDREN'S CHARITIES, EMPLOYEE ASSISTANCE PROGRAMS, AND ALCOHOL ABUSE PREVENTION PROGRAMS.

BROWN DISTRIBUTING COMPANY EMPLOYS MORE THAN 150 PEOPLE AND RUNS A FLEET OF 125 TRUCKS IN THE GREATER RICHMOND AREA.

TODAY, THE BROWN BROTHERS' BUSINESS SERVES SOME 2,000 RETAILERS THROUGHOUT CENTRAL VIRGINIA.

$\mathcal{C}$USTOMERS WHO NEED FINISHED PRODUCTS IN ALUMINUM, steel, stainless steel, brass, or copper have come to Cushing Manufacturing Company in South Richmond for more than 40 years. This homegrown metal fabricating company has built a reputation in the region and across the nation by consistently meeting customers' needs on time and on budget. ❧ Since it opened for business in 1957, Cushing has

been turning raw materials into finished products to the specifications of government agencies, businesses, and industries. Through the years, the company has amassed a wealth of experience, applying it to metals in its state-of-the-art production and manufacturing plant to meet clients' most precise specifications.

With about 50 employees and a full range of equipment including CNC punches; CNC plasma; CNC press brakes; welding, burning, fabricating, and finishing equipment; and the latest manufacturing computer software, Cushing has developed a business with sales that amount to about $5 million annually. Today, the privately held business is one of the nation's leading manufacturers of tollbooths. "We started the tollbooth business about 30 years ago, when we won a contract to supply booths for the new Downtown Expressway in Richmond," says Ross Jennings, who has been with the company since 1966 and serves today as its president.

The company counts among its clients the Virginia Department of Transportation, North Texas Tollway Authority, Harris County Toll Road Authority, Pennsylvania Turnpike, Maryland Transportation Authority, Richmond Metropolitan Airport,

and the Delaware Department of Transportation.

But Cushing provides much more than tollbooths. It also is a leading producer of precision fabricated sheet metal products such as cabinets, countertops, enclosures, and UL-rated junction boxes. Whether a client needs a single item or thousands of units that are exactly alike, Cushing can do the job.

And the company is skilled at tank trailer repair and rebuilding. Cushing is a registered ASME "R" stamp facility, capable of doing DOT inspections and certifications. Cushing maintains a large inventory of parts in order to provide customers with prompt service. The company also has worked extensively with clients in the construction, tobacco, electronics, utilities, and food processing industries.

Being in the Right Place

According to Jennings, his hometown of Richmond has been an ideal place for the business to grow, adapt, and change. The company is situated in the middle of one of the nation's busiest shipping routes. Heavily used rail lines, Richmond's port, and the interstate are all close by. And some of the region's largest and longest-standing industrial operations, including Philip Morris, DuPont, and Honeywell, are neighbors and clients.

"We've grown and changed quite a bit over the years," says Jennings. "I can't imagine us being in a better place. Here, we can build a solid business that should continue to do well far into the Richmond region's promising future."

FROM TOLLBOOTH AND U.L.-APPROVED JUNCTION AND PULL BOX CONSTRUCTION TO A VARIETY OF FINISHED PRODUCTS IN ALUMINUM, STEEL, STAINLESS STEEL, BRASS, OR COPPER, CUSHING MANUFACTURING COMPANY HAS BEEN THE COMPANY OF CHOICE IN SOUTH RICHMOND FOR MORE THAN 40 YEARS.

FOR MORE THAN A DECADE, UKROP'S SUPER MARKETS, INC. HAS been the dominant grocery retailer in the Richmond area. The company's place in the community is more prominent than sales figures alone indicate. This homegrown business, still owned and operated by the Ukrop family, is as much a part of Richmond as Monument Avenue, the Virginia capitol, and the mighty James River. ∞ With more than 5,500 associates, Ukrop's is one of metro Richmond's largest employers. For more than a decade, it has owned more than a 30 percent share of the region's grocery business, despite considerable competition from national and regional supermarket heavyweights. Ukrop's success has been built on a formula that includes high quality; innovations in services, products, and facilities; and an unusually deep commitment to community.

"For more than 64 years, our company has striven to create a brand that supports us and that stands for trust, integrity, and commitment to excellence," says Jim Ukrop, chairman.

A Firm Foundation

Joe and Jacquelin Ukrop opened the first Ukrop's in South Richmond in 1937, after Joe's father mortgaged the family farm to finance the new business. Setting the service standard that would come to typify Ukrop's, the Ukrops served each customer personally—going so far as to offer credit and delivery. By the 1950s, the store included a full lunch counter and was one of the highest-volume supermarkets around.

The addition into the business of the Ukrops' son Jim in the 1960s and their son Bobby in the 1970s helped Ukrop's expand and open new stores, while maintaining its commitment to superior service and high-quality foods. The 1980s and 1990s saw expansion to Petersburg, Colonial Heights, Fredericksburg, and Williamsburg, and a continuing gain in market share. Now, some 27 Ukrop's stores operate in central Virginia.

An Industry Leader

Ukrop's has been out front on successful trends, and the company's response to changing lifestyle dynamics has been just as important in building a loyal clientele. To reward loyal customers, in 1987 Ukrop's launched its Ukrop's Valued Customer Program, which offers in-store electronic discounts. Widely copied, the Ukrop's program was the first such program in the nation.

Since 1989, Ukrop's has offered an expanding line of fresh, chilled, prepared foods in response to customer lifestyle changes. In addition, the company has begun putting now-popular grills and cafés in its stores. Today, food service areas account for up to 11 percent of the business in many stores, and that percentage is expected to grow.

Recognizing the relationship between health and food, Ukrop's began putting pharmacies into its stores in 1989, but the firm's commitment to health didn't stop there. The company now sponsors health screening and counseling programs, and the *Live Healthy and Be Healthy* show on local cable TV, which focuses on health-related issues and discusses Ukrop's growing inventory of natural and organic products.

In 1997, as banks around the nation were consolidating, eliminating local institutions people had relied on for years, Ukrop's teamed up with National Commerce Bank Corporation to create First Market Bank, the first supermarket-owned bank in the nation. Currently, there are 17 First Market Bank branches inside stores and another six freestanding branches in the metro Richmond area. Operating with Ukrop's high-quality, high-service

JACQUELIN AND JOE UKROP, ALONG WITH THEIR SONS JIM AND BOBBY, ENSURE THAT UKROP'S SUPER MARKETS, INC. CONTINUES TO REMAIN A VITAL PART OF THE RICHMOND COMMUNITY, WHERE IT HAS BEEN A FAMILY BUSINESS SINCE 1937.

ADDING A MODERN TOUCH, MANY UKROP'S NOW FEATURE A GRILL AND CAFÉ.

orientation, the bank has proved to be another success story.

Good Neighbors

"Our company believes in supporting the community that supports us, and that is why we contribute a minimum of 10 percent of our profits each year," says Jim Ukrop. "We believe investing in our community through our charitable giving program is not only the right thing to do, but makes good business sense."

Through Ukrop's vision, mission, and shared values statement, all associates are encouraged to commit themselves to improving the lives of their families and community, a philosophy to which the company's founders adhere. During World War II, Ukrop's closed on Wednesday afternoons so Joe Ukrop and his workers could help area farmers with their crops. In the 1950s, Ukrop's began supporting youth sports leagues, and the company's associates are now involved in activities with United Way, Ukrop's/Retail Merchants Association Christmas Parade, American Heart Walk, and blood drives with the Virginia Bold Services. Many Ukrop's associates and their children take advantage of company benefits that include continuing education opportunities and scholarships.

Since Ukrop's 50th anniversary in 1987, the company has contributed 2 percent of a customer's total spending during a 13-week period to a charity of his or her choice through Ukrop's Golden Gift Program. Over the years, the program has raised more than $8 million for some 5,000 local nonprofit organizations.

Ukrop's has been recognized with the American Business Ethics Award, the Better Business Bureau's Torch Award for marketplace integrity, and the Brotherhood Award presented by the American Conference of Christians and Jews. In 2000, and again in 2001, the company was named by *Fortune Magazine* as one of the best 100 companies to work for in America.

Into the 21st Century

Ukrop's Super Markets, Inc. plans to grow and expand in the new millennium according to its successful formula: new, delicious foods will be added; stores and other facilities will be remodeled and built, with attention paid to improved service; and associates and customers will be treated fairly.

"We have now entered the 21st century, and as we continue our focus on being innovative and staying one step ahead of the latest trends, superior customer service will remain our number one priority," Bobby Ukrop says. "After all, a golden principle does not tarnish with age."

FROM FRESH-BACKED BAGELS TO THE ANNUAL EMPLOYEE PICNIC, UKROP'S IS COMMITTED TO BOTH ITS CUSTOMERS AND ITS EMPLOYEES.

WTVR-TV

Central Virginia from its landmark tower in Richmond, WTVR-TV has built a reputation over the years for dependability and community involvement. Often referred to as "the South's first television station," WTVR produces more than 26 hours a week of programming that is seen in some 475,000 households. ⌇ The station's coverage spans a

region that reaches from Fredericksburg to the north, westward beyond Charlottesville, east into Tidewater, and south into North Carolina. It is a region of challenging size and diversity, and the WTVR staff strives to meet that challenge with award-winning work.

First Then, First Now

WTVR signed on the air April 22, 1948, two years after Wilbur Havens filed a petition with the Federal Communications Commission that brought him the first television license south of the Mason-Dixon Line. During the 1950s, Havens built a tower behind WTVR's West Broad Street headquarters, which he christened in 1954 as "a beacon to all those entering Richmond." At 1,049 feet above sea level, it was the largest freestanding structure in the country at the time. The tower stands today as a familiar city landmark.

WTVR was sold to Roy H. Park Broadcasting in 1965. In 1997, Raycom Media Inc., a company with 35 stations from Puerto Rico to Hawaii, bought the station. Raycom is unusual in this era of corporate mergers and takeovers in that television is its sole business. The company is run by people who have built careers operating television stations and managing newsrooms. The Raycom network is linked by an intranet so that information, broadcasts, and stories can be shared when events warrant.

Focus on News

"News is our focus, and local news is what defines us," says Mark Pimentel, vice president and general manager of WTVR. As a CBS affiliate, the station has won numerous Emmy awards, along with honors from the Virginia Association of Broadcasters and the Associated Press, including Outstand-

ing News Operation and Best In-Depth Reporting. WTVR alumni have gone on to work at ABC, CBS, and CNN, while the 55-person news staff includes experienced professionals with long-standing ties to the community, as well as younger staffers who bring energy and new ideas to the newsroom.

WTVR has made a multimillion-dollar investment in equipment for its new newsroom. Furnished with the latest computer equipment, the newsroom will provide a unique, exciting venue for newscasts. It also will provide WTVR with the tools it needs as the digital broadcasting era opens in 2002.

In keeping with the advance of technology, WTVR has also launched itself onto the Internet with a site at www.WTVR.com. The Web presence enables people anywhere in the world to keep in touch with Richmond news, sports, weather, and entertainment via computer. The site features the most current local news along with WTVR programming information. And it gives viewers access to the station's Doppler radar, which is updated minute by minute.

Responding to Weather Emergencies

Research shows that weather is the first reason viewers turn on local news. And, in a region like the one surround-

FROM ITS ORIGINAL NEWS STUDIO (RIGHT) TO THE DOPPLER MAX 6 WEATHER RADAR, WTVR-TV HAS BEEN A NEWS LEADER IN RICHMOND FOR MORE THAN 50 YEARS.

STEPHANIE ROCHON AND RAY COLLINS ANCHOR THE NEWS FROM THE NEWS 6 NEWSROOM.

ing Richmond, which has been struck in recent years by hurricanes, floods, ice storms, and droughts, weather reporting may be even more important.

To respond quickly and professionally to weather emergencies, WTVR has put into place StormTeam 6. Headed by staff meteorologists, the team also calls on top news reporters when necessary.

In addition to manpower, the station has invested in a 100-foot tower equipped with DopplerMax 6, the most powerful television radar system in Virginia. At 250,000 watts, it allows staff meteorologists and viewers alike to view weather systems across the state of Virginia and throughout the region. This digital radar and computer imaging presents storms in three dimensions for greater detail and more accuracy. It can identify dangerous features, including wind shear and tornadoes.

WTVR shares its state-of-the-art weather information with emergency services personnel in the city of Richmond and surrounding counties. It also makes the data available to state emergency services officials and to Richmond International Airport. And when hurricanes swept along the East Coast, the station worked with other Raycom stations in Savannah and Wilmington on coverage.

Commitment to Community

The Richmond community is diverse and challenging to cover, but the station is up to the task. Although it has been greatly expanded over the years, WTVR's headquarters remains at the same West Broad location where it started in 1948, just minutes from Richmond City Hall and the Virginia State Capitol.

With its For Kids Sake program, which was started in 1985, WTVR has donated untold hours of airtime on its news programs, in public service announcements, and on fund-raising telethons to issues like parenting, children's mental health, education, and services. And, with community support, the station has spent $750,000 to build 19 tot lots throughout the community, many of them in underserved communities.

WTVR also holds regular meetings with its Black Advisory Council to make sure it is attuned to the concerns of Richmond's African-American community. The station provides three college scholarships each year to minority students from the area. Recently, one of those scholarship winners came back to work at WTVR as an executive news producer, bringing the program full circle.

"We seek to reach a real cross-section of our community," says Pimentel. "We have remained in the city of Richmond for years, and we're proud to be here."

ℱOR MANY, THE MOST-WELCOME WAKE-UP CALL IN CENTRAL Virginia is the sound of the NBC chimes ringing in *NBC12 News Today*. Each weekday morning starting at 5, Andrea McDaniel and Mark Hubbard preside at the news desk, with Ben Woods in the First Warning Weather Center and Yvonne Nelson in the First Warning Traffic Center, helping people in the Richmond area to begin their day. And they do so

successfully. More than 50 percent of the morning news viewers choose WWBT/NBC12 each weekday.

One reason for the show's popularity is WWBT's Sky 12–Richmond's only television news helicopter–which brings live traffic reports, complete with an exclusive view of any unusual road conditions or delays, to commuters.

At 5 p.m., Sky 12 returns for the afternoon commute, combining its efforts with Richmond's number one news team. Gene Lepley and Sabrina Squire kick it off at 5 for a first look at the day's news. Gene Cox joins Squire at 5:30, 6, and 11 p.m. for up-to-the-minute newscasts. Together with meteorologist Jim Duncan and sports anchor Ben Hamlin, Cox and Squire are the longest-running, most-watched anchor team in Central Virginia.

WWBT/NBC12 signed on from its landmark, state-of-the-art facility on Midlothian Turnpike in 1956, with a 15-minute newscast. Since 1968, the station has been operated by Jefferson Pilot Communications, which has continuously upgraded the station's facilities and staff, creating a consistent source of reliable information. Throughout its existence, the station has been one of America's most powerful local television stations. And for the past decade, WWBT has held the

top spot as Richmond's most-watched station for news.

On Your Side

It all begins with NBC12's slogan: On Your Side. This promise to Richmond viewers means that the station intends always to be on their side with news, information, and even a helping hand when needed. That mission has served the station well for more than 15 years.

Reaching out to the community is what NBC12 is all about, says Don Richards, the station's vice president and general manager. Since making this commitment, tens of thousands of area residents have been served by Call 12 volunteers or other community partners who provide assistance in a wide variety of ways. From NBC12 health initiatives, in which the station

works with area hospitals to provide free medical services, to the annual Salvation Army Angel Tree campaign, which makes Christmas brighter for area children, NBC12 works to make a difference in the community.

Maintaining and keeping the On Your Side promise in a high-tech world means expanding beyond NBC12's four and one-half hours of daily local news to provide constant access to news and information through telephone and on-line resources. The station provides fully interactive connections to viewers through its phone line and the station's services are also easily accessible using the newest communications pipeline–www.nbc12.com.

By using these connections, viewers have no trouble finding out more information on news reports, getting

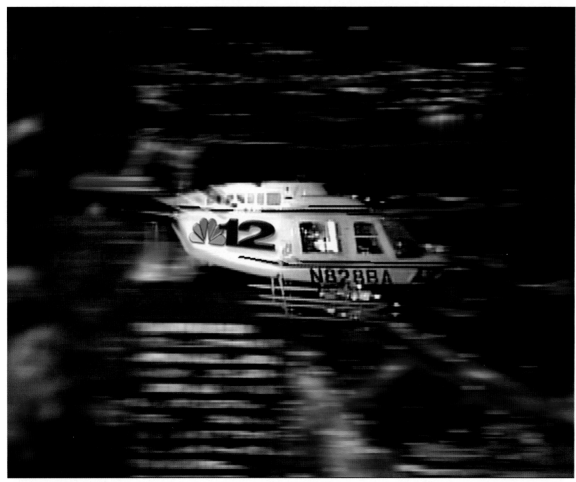

answers to their questions, or receiving help with consumer problems. These connections also provide a valuable link to the station by allowing viewers to talk about issues and concerns that affect their lives.

First in Weather

If a television station is to serve the community above and beyond daily news, and remain as the viewers' first choice, it must be first in weather reporting. NBC12's First Warning Weather Team, a group of experienced meteorologists led by Jim Duncan, is number one with Richmond viewers. First Warning Weather far and away exceeds any other source in Central Virginia, providing around-the-clock watches and warnings—and, if needed, continuous weather coverage and closings during severe winter storms and hurricanes.

Each year, the station's commitment to weather forecasting has grown, both in expertise and in the use of the most advanced weather technology available. NBC12 was the first in Richmond to launch Doppler radar and now, with the station's latest upgrade, NBC12 can track approaching storms from even farther away, allowing the weather team to give viewers increasingly accurate and dependable forecasts. First Warning Weather Service also provides real-time

conditions via NBC12's WeatherNet, which consists of 40 neighborhood weather stations reporting conditions both on the air and on-line.

Committed to Quality

In addition to being Richmond's first choice for news and weather, NBC12 also takes pride in its entertainment offerings. Through its NBC partnership, the station presents popular, award-winning drama and comedy series, along with sporting events ranging from the Olympics to NBA basketball to major golf tournaments. In addition, NBC12 is the exclusive home in the region for other number-one-rated programs, including *Entertainment*

Tonight and *The Oprah Winfrey Show*. All this programming provides a unique, high-quality environment for advertisers. The station's sales and marketing department is a major resource of sophisticated research, and it ensures marketing advantages for local and national advertisers.

"In so many ways, WWBT's promise of being on the side of viewers in Richmond and beyond has broadened, and is constantly being refined as the communities of Central Virginia continue to grow and flourish," says Richards. "As we embark on a new era of continuing change, one thing remains the same—NBC12's commitment to quality and our community."

David R. McGeorge Car Company, Inc.

In Richmond, a city where tradition is valuable currency, the McGeorge name is well established in the minds of car buyers. For more than 40 years, three generations of the McGeorge family have sold automobiles to generations of clients who rely on the dealerships for quality vehicles, dependable service, and personal attention. ⁓ The first McGeorge dealerships were founded in 1957 by David R. McGeorge,

who sold used cars from a lot on West Broad Street. His son Robert L. McGeorge took over the business and oversaw much of its growth to what it is today. Rod McGeorge, the third generation, oversees the operations of two McGeorge dealerships today.

In 2001, McGeorge Toyota sold some 2,000 new cars. The Mercedes dealership, which carries the David R. McGeorge name, will sell approximately 600. Both are among the elite dealers for their brands; both are number one in central Virginia.

While sales figures may be a convenient measure of a dealership's success, it is not the measure the McGeorges apply first to their business. Following the strong lead set by Robert McGeorge, Rod McGeorge emphasizes that "what we have here is a family business. My grandfather started it. It has meant the world to my father, and that's the way we are going to operate. We intend to treat our clients and our employees like family, which keeps them happy and loyal."

Surrounded by Good People
Since 1960, David R. McGeorge Car Company, Inc. has been a successful Mercedes-Benz dealership. In 1968, the company acquired a Toyota

franchise, and McGeorge sold both nameplates from its West Broad Street location. It has focused exclusively on those two brands since 1985. Sales grew to the point where, in 1998, McGeorge moved the Mercedes dealership to its own new facility on Broad, and the original facility now carries the Toyota dealership.

Both of the McGeorge dealerships have been recognized repeatedly for providing the high-quality service their clients want. McGeorge Toyota has won Toyota's Presidents Award five years in a row, in recognition of its distinction in service, parts, and sales combined.

McGeorge gives credit for much of this success to the company's 160 employees, many of whom have been with the company for more than a decade—and a few of whom date to the era when the business' founder still ran the place. When his father defined the car company as a family business, he included in that family the people who worked there as well as their clients.

Keeping Them Coming Back
In the car business, service is the key. "We sell very fine automobiles, but any car will have problems," Rod McGeorge says. "Taking care

SINCE 1957, THE NAME DAVID R. MCGEORGE CAR COMPANY, INC. HAS BEEN SYNONYMOUS WITH QUALITY IN THE GREATER RICHMOND MARKET. GUIDING THE FIRM TODAY ARE (FROM LEFT) ROD MCGEORGE—REPRESENTING THE THIRD GENERATION OF THE MCGEORGE FAMILY—AND HIS FATHER, ROBERT L. MCGEORGE.

of these problems is essential."

One key to solving problems to clients' satisfaction is the team of experienced assistant service managers on hand at the dealerships' service departments. Part of their job is to let customers know everything that's going on with their cars during service calls so there is no guessing, no surprise.

As one client said in a recent survey, "They correct the little things upon request. Nothing is insignificant if it's important to me." One indication that this approach to service has been successful, says McGeorge, is that people come back. It's not unusual to have parents who own a McGeorge car bring their children to one of the dealerships when time comes to buy them a car.

Mercedes and Toyota, like most automakers, take surveys of buyers and rate dealerships on their customer satisfaction index. The McGeorge dealerships always score in the top percentile, well above Mercedes and Toyota standards.

Keeping Pace with Change

McGeorge recently celebrated its 40th year as a Mercedes dealer and 30th as a Toyota dealership. That's unusual longevity for any dealer with any brand, especially in the modern era of mega-dealerships.

As the industry sees more and more consolidation, the McGeorge dealerships will continue to be places where clients who have needs "can walk in my door and talk to me about it," McGeorge says. "By doing this we feel we can keep our clients in the McGeorge family for years to come."

But McGeorge says this personal approach must be combined with the use of state-of-the-art technology that is increasingly important with today's sophisticated automobiles, and with more demanding clients. The McGeorge dealerships' service facilities are equipped with the latest computerized diagnostic equipment, and the people who work there are skilled at using this equipment. And with the Internet growing as a source of

information and even sales, both dealerships have sales people designated to handle inquiries that come in through the business' Web site.

A Family Tradition

For clients, family and employees, McGeorge is like home. There's a photo on the wall at McGeorge Toyota of a grandfather, his son, and his grandson all standing beside cars they bought and have serviced at the dealership. Inside the dealerships, there are several father-and-son combinations and a mother-and-daughter combination of employees, some of whom work side by side. Rod McGeorge says this is a source of pride within the business, which values family, tradition, and good work.

"We're going to do the best we can to take care of the clients," he says. And while the business will continue to grow, it won't grow so large that it is no longer a family business, beneficial and enjoyable for both clients and employees.

McGEORGE RECENTLY CELEBRATED ITS 40TH YEAR AS A MERCEDES DEALER AND 30TH AS A TOYOTA DEALERSHIP. THAT'S UNUSUAL LONGEVITY FOR ANY DEALER, ESPECIALLY IN THE MODERN ERA OF MEGA-DEALERSHIPS.

McGEORGE TOYOTA HAS WON TOYOTA'S PRESIDENTS AWARD FIVE YEARS IN A ROW, IN RECOGNITION OF ITS DISTINCTION IN SERVICE, PARTS, AND SALES COMBINED.

Virginia Sprinkler Company, Inc.

VSC

VIRGINIA SPRINKLER COMPANY, INC., FOUNDED JUST NORTH of Richmond in 1958 by Roland C. Giles and V.M. Buck, has grown to be one of the nation's largest fire protection companies. With current sales exceeding $50 million, Virginia Sprinkler was included in the 2000 edition of *Contractor* magazine's Book of Giants list as one of the top 10 fire protection contractors in the nation. ⌘ The company's original offices were in Giles' house north of Richmond, also the boyhood home of Martin L.

FOUNDED IN 1958, VIRGINIA SPRINKLER COMPANY, INC. IS TODAY ONE OF THE TOP 10 FIRE PROTECTION COMPANIES IN THE NATION.

FROM DOWNTOWN HIGH-RISES TO SUBURBAN APARTMENT COMPLEXES, VIRGINIA SPRINKLER CAN HELP PROTECT VIRTUALLY ANY TYPE OF STRUCTURE.

Giles, son of the founder and president and owner of the company since 1972. This original building was expanded several times as the business grew, but was demolished in 1999 to make way for a modern, new building that houses the Richmond division and the offices of VSC Corporation, Virginia Sprinkler's parent company.

VSC's new, 32,000-square-foot office/warehouse building opened on the site in 2000. The building includes office and warehouse space for the Richmond division—accommodating its designers, administrative and sales staff, alarm technicians, and inspection department. A large training facility allows space for apprenticeship and other technical training classes.

Offering Broader Services

In 1968, Virginia Sprinkler opened its first expansion office in Springfield, Virginia, to serve the growing northern Virginia and Washington, D.C., markets. Since then, the company has added offices in Virginia Beach and Salem, Virginia, and Baltimore.

In 1990, to reflect the broader services provided by the company, VSC Corporation was formed as the holding company of the organization. Today, VSC Corporation is made up of Virginia Sprinkler; Virginia Pipe and Supply Company, a supply and fabrication facility; Virginia Fire Protection

Company, which specializes in alarm systems and special hazard work; and Beta Systems of Virginia Inc., a Chesapeake-based firm acquired in 1998 that specializes in fire alarm, nurse-call, sound, and security and access systems.

Virginia Sprinkler and its subsidiaries design, install, maintain, and inspect all the systems installed for a wide variety of new construction and renovation projects throughout the mid-Atlantic region. The company is best known for its fire sprinkler systems, but the firm also provides a full range of fire and life safety protection applications, including foam water, special FM200 gas systems, fire alarm and detection systems, closed-circuit security systems, access systems, nurse-call systems, special hazard systems, and inspection services.

Virginia Sprinkler has demonstrated its expertise in projects such as office buildings, warehouses, retail sites, institutional buildings, multifamily residential structures, and industrial buildings. The company has installed security and fire protection systems in high-rise towers, convention centers, and shopping malls. Virginia Sprinkler's tradition of excellence has led to the company's selection as a preferred vendor in the Virginia Health Care Association.

Clients such as Circuit City, Capital One, Health South Medical Center, and Virginia State Library rely on Virginia Sprinkler's expertise for their fire protection needs. Known for its work in renovation and retrofit installations, the company has been entrusted with fire protection work on historical properties such as St. John's Church

in Richmond, the site of Patrick Henry's famous "Give me liberty or give me death" speech, and, most recently, the Virginia Governor's Mansion.

Culture of Quality

Virginia Sprinkler has been built on a culture that emphasizes strong ethical principles and personal bonds, Martin Giles says. The company takes pride in the solid financial reputation it enjoys among suppliers and clients. VSC also takes pride in the quality of its workforce of more than 500 skilled workers, many of whom have been with the company from its beginning.

The VSC staff includes an in-house fire protection professional engineer, as well as National Institute for Certification in Engineering Technologies (NICET) Certified Level III and IV design personnel. VSC relies on sophisticated computer-aided design (CAD) technology. Service and inspection departments provide 24-hour service with guaranteed response time, and offer warranted work and computerized tracking for inspections. The company also provides an approved apprenticeship program, as well as safety and training programs.

This well-trained, experienced workforce enables the company to respond to exceptional production and scheduling requirements that may arise. "I recognize that our success has been based on the quality of our work, and the level of service provided by our talented and dedicated employees," Giles says.

Diverse Areas of Leadership

Virginia Sprinkler extends its work into the community by supporting a variety of causes such as the burn unit at the Medical College of Virginia Hospitals. The company's classroom facility is made available for fire safety programs, and the firm supports local school districts in their career planning efforts with the young people of the metropolitan area. At the local level, Giles is a member of the Hanover Tavern Association, Hanover Education Foundation, and Hospital Hospitality House.

The leadership of Virginia Sprinkler's senior management in the fire protection industry extends beyond the company through their active involvement in the America Fire Sprinkler Association, National

Fire Protection Association, and other industry organizations.

Today, Virginia Sprinkler and its subsidiaries offer complete fire protection systems, and the company is well equipped to handle any project from the estimate through to the completed installation. With more than 40 years of experience in the fire protection industry, the company maintains its role as a leader in customer service, technology, and vision.

1962   Hewlett-Packard Company

1963   Leonard W. Lambert & Associates

1965   Richmond Montessori School

1967   James River Heating and Air Conditioning

1967   The Restaurant Company

1968   Virginia Commonwealth University

1969   W.J. Rapp Company, Inc.

1972   Colonial Mechanical Corporation

1974   Ralph L. Samuels & Assoc.

1975   Crews & Hancock, P.L.C.

1975   KBS, Inc.

1975   Regency Square

1975   Westminster-Canterbury Richmond

1977   Woodfin Oil

Hewlett-Packard Company

HEWLETT-PACKARD COMPANY (HP) CAME TO RICHMOND LONG before personal computers and ink-jet printers became established features of businesses and homes. The technology revolution since then has led to a thriving relationship between business and community. Today, Hewlett-Packard operates from four main locations in the area, developing, manufacturing, distributing, and selling a broad range of its products. At the same time, the company's operations have helped create thousands of jobs in the

area, and its commitment to the community includes long-reaching educational programs that promise to enhance the quality of life in central Virginia well into the future.

Hewlett-Packard came to Richmond in 1962 and soon built a sales office that serves central Virginia and employs about 60 people, according to Dan Ross, mid-Atlantic sales manager for HP. That location's success helped the company pinpoint Richmond as an attractive site based on its proximity to huge eastern markets and the relatively low cost of space and the high quality of workers available. "We've invested heavily here because we've been successful here," says Ross.

In the 1990s, with the computer-driven economy in high gear, the company opened manufacturing operations at Rivers Bend near Enon and White Oak–near Richmond International Airport–along with a huge distribution center, also at White Oak. Today, Hewlett-Packard products such as printers, cartridges, and special media papers are shipped all over the world after passing through Richmond on their way to market.

Helping Develop the Workforce of the Future
"Hewlett-Packard has always worked to participate in communities where it has operations," says Jan McDaniel, Richmond site facilities manager.

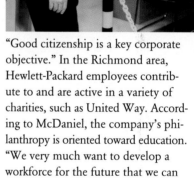

"Good citizenship is a key corporate objective." In the Richmond area, Hewlett-Packard employees contribute to and are active in a variety of charities, such as United Way. According to McDaniel, the company's philanthropy is oriented toward education. "We very much want to develop a workforce for the future that we can tap," McDaniel says.

Hewlett-Packard provides mentors for students at the Governors School in Petersburg, which specializes in technology education. The company also provided a grant to supply the school with printing equipment. Grants have also been made to Clover Hill High School for Science and Mathematics. Recently, Hewlett-Packard joined John Tyler Community College to help the growing school in booming Chesterfield County produce

workers who will succeed in the business world of the future.

"We are interested in targeting our philanthropy to get the maximum bang for the buck," McDaniel says. "We believe education is the way we can do that."

Pilot Programs Help Plot Future
As Hewlett-Packard grows, the company seeks ways of streamlining its business, and the Richmond operations are at the heart of that process, according to Ross. Because the company is represented in Richmond in almost all aspects of its work, the region has played a key role in HP's pilot effort to integrate processes that efficiently serve business and consumer customers.

"We are trying to put all these functions under one roof, with a manager there who can represent all HP products and services," Ross says. "Businesses and people must make decisions in a short time now. We are trying to invent new ways to help them do this. And with so much growth taking place in the mid-Atlantic region, and Richmond right in the middle of it, it's a very good place for us to pilot this program. We'll be rolling these integrated teams out across the nation in the future, and Richmond will have been the place that let us know it works."

HEWLETT-PACKARD COMPANY (HP) CAME TO RICHMOND LONG BEFORE PERSONAL COMPUTERS AND INK-JET PRINTERS BECAME ESTABLISHED FEATURES OF BUSINESSES AND HOMES. THE TECHNOLOGY REVOLUTION SINCE THEN HAS LED TO A THRIVING RELATIONSHIP BETWEEN BUSINESS AND COMMUNITY.

AT LEONARD W. LAMBERT AND ASSOCIATES, THE HALLS OF justice and the halls of home sweet home seem to be one and the same—at least for the junior partners. The Richmond law firm Lambert and Associates is composed of founding partner Leonard W. Lambert, his daughter Linda Lambert Anderson, and his son Brice E. Lambert. Since the firm bears his family name, the senior Lambert says that service to his clients and

his community comes with a personal guarantee of absolute commitment in the areas of personal injury, real estate, criminal, and civil law.

"We are a family law firm dedicated to providing the highest level of services and attention to our customers so that they feel comfortable coming to us for any of their legal services," Lambert says.

A Legacy of Law and Public Service

Lambert, a native Richmonder, began practicing law in September 1963 after receiving his law degree from Howard University. Among Lambert's earliest law associates was former Virginia Governor L. Douglas Wilder, who was just beginning his trek through an extensive career in public service. During his own four-decade career, Lambert has established himself as one of the most noted names in Richmond's legal community, as well as one of its leading public servants.

In 1973, Lambert became the first minority appointed as a substitute judge for the general district courts in the Greater Richmond area. And while he serves his community at some of the top levels of the local legal system, Lambert offers the assistance and prestige of his firm to many other causes and concerns throughout Richmond.

The list of institutions to which Lambert has offered his time and energy in official roles includes the Greater Richmond Chamber of Commerce, Metro Leadership Richmond, the Virginia State Board for Community Colleges, the American Red Cross, the Children's Home Society, the Jewish Community Center, the Young Men's Christian Association, and the Greater Richmond Transit Company.

"Our greatest pride, I think, is the work we have done with the Garfield Memorial Children's Fund," Lambert says. Lambert was part of the group that founded the fund in the late 1980s in support of a program that provides tutoring for children in Richmond's

public housing sectors. In exchange for the tutoring, students volunteer assistance to elderly residents in public housing.

An Open Door for Young Lawyers

The concept of service and education is something Lambert takes seriously, especially when it comes to helping young lawyers, even those who are not of his own flesh and blood. "My door is always open to young lawyers to give them advice and counseling," Lambert says. "We have provided many

opportunities for young lawyers to come to our firm and learn about the law and advance their careers. Several have become judges and so forth."

With the additions to his firm of his daughter in 1997 and his son in 1998, Lambert has been able to broaden the counseling of young lawyers within his own family and hopes the firm will not stop there. "We've been providing legal services in Richmond for more than 38 years," he says, "and we're going to continue to expand and grow."

THE RICHMOND LAW FIRM OF LEONARD W. LAMBERT AND ASSOCIATES IS A FAMILY FIRM WHOSE PRINCIPALS ARE (FROM LEFT) FOUNDER LEONARD W. LAMBERT, DAUGHTER LINDA LAMBERT ANDERSON, AND SON BRICE E. LAMBERT.

RICHMOND MONTESSORI SCHOOL WAS FOUNDED IN 1965 TO provide children in central Virginia with a creative, responsive learning environment that nurtures each child to reach his or her fullest potential. ✷ The Montessori approach is summed up on a plaque in the school's main building: "I hear and I forget. I see and I remember. I do and I understand." Based on educational methods developed in 1907 by

Dr. Maria Montessori, Italy's first female physician, students are taught in a classroom atmosphere where they become self-motivated, self-assured, and respectful, while gaining a love of learning.

The school, accredited by the American Montessori Society, enrolls approximately 300 children, ranging in age from 30 months to 14 years. A high-quality preschool education is offered, which research shows is the basis for later achievement and helps to prepare the child for the challenges of adolescence and beyond.

A Place for Creative Thinking

Richmond Montessori School takes pride in the environment provided to its students. Set back from Parham Road by a wooded buffer and a stream in Richmond's West End, the school's gray stone-and-glass building surrounds a welcoming lobby, affectionately referred to as "the silo," which is capped by a skylight roof.

Each of the school's classrooms, enhanced by large, attractive windows, opens onto a garden cared for by the children. Students work singly or in small groups in their multiage classes. The modern technology center, used in the elementary and middle school grades, is located in the newly renovated library/media center, and links students and faculty to global resources.

THE RICHMOND MONTESSORI SCHOOL APPROACH IS SUMMED UP ON A PLAQUE IN THE SCHOOL'S MAIN BUILDING: "I HEAR AND I FORGET. I SEE AND I REMEMBER. I DO AND I UNDERSTAND."

The Montessori curriculum is organized as a spiral of integrated studies rather than as a traditional, linear model in which the curriculum is compartmentalized into separate subjects. Lessons are introduced simply and concretely, through the use of materials, in the early years, and are reintroduced several times over the following years with increasing degrees of abstraction and complexity. Montessori uses an integrated, thematic approach that ties together all areas of the curriculum. This integrated approach is one of Montessori's greatest strengths. With a lead teacher and an assistant, a low student-teacher ratio is maintained. The core curriculum is enriched at all grades through music, Spanish, physical education, and art.

Developing Mutual Respect

At the entrance to Richmond Montessori School, an International Flag Garden has been established—helping to symbolize the many countries and cultures, as well as the diverse community, that attend the school. "Diversity is what the children will find in their world," Sandra Johnson, director of admissions, says. "Our families want diversity, and it's the essence of who we are." Diversity in the school population is due in part to the success of Montessori schools worldwide. Students have come to the school from Belgium, Great Britain, France, Hong Kong, Italy, Mexico, and India, as well as other countries and localities.

Members of Richmond's increasingly cosmopolitan society know they can depend on a Montessori education to provide a high-quality learning environment for their children. The educational experience provided by Richmond Montessori School sets the cornerstone for the student to succeed in life and anywhere in the world.

WITH MORE THAN 30 YEARS IN THE FIELD AS A COMMERCIAL and industrial general contractor, W.J. Rapp Company, Inc. stands by its motto: Together we achieve the extraordinary. The company has built a reputation in central Virginia for high-quality work, peak performance on the job, and ethical dealings with customers. Working across Richmond's varied business landscape, as well as other areas of Virginia and out-of-state locations, W.J. Rapp Company provides support, maintenance, and general contracting services. These services are offered to transportation providers, food processors, airports, communications companies, retail and automotive firms, manufacturers, banks, and hospitals, as well as state and local government.

W.J. Rapp Company's client list includes small businesses, home owners, and Fortune 500 companies such as Nabisco, Philip Morris, DuPont, Federal Reserve Bank, Richmond Marriott Hotel, Virginia Power, and Ukrop's Super Markets. While the company has been involved in high-visibility jobs in the region, "We're not often what you'll see," says Dennis Rapp, president and owner. "But a lot of what you see is built on what we do."

Building a Reputation

Already having more than 15 years' experience in the construction business, W.J. Rapp Jr. began running this small concrete contracting operation out of his apartment when he founded the company in 1969. Since then, the company has grown steadily. "People came to know my work and to trust me," says Rapp, who is still involved in the business.

In 1978, Rapp turned the operation of the company over to his son Dennis, who then bought the business in 1986. During that period, W.J. Rapp Company expanded, taking on more commercial projects. In 1988, the company moved into its current office located in a heavily industrialized area of Richmond, south of the James River near Interstate 95. This location has proved to be a good one, readily accessible to many clients.

Quick and Dependable

Today, quick response and dependable, quality work are the hallmarks of W.J. Rapp Company. By owning and maintaining its own equipment, the company is able to offer quality control, modify equipment, and provide filtering and cleaning systems to fit clients' needs for specialized uses. This is particularly important when working in food services, drug processing, and other areas.

W.J. Rapp Company also works in fields like plant maintenance, emergency services, renovations, general commercial construction, building additions, conversions, and demolition. The company also works on plumbing jobs, performs concrete work, and builds and repairs swimming pools and Jacuzzis.

People Solving Problems

With a core of skilled workers, W.J. Rapp Company is known for flexibility and creativity in solving problems. "People who work here share responsibilities," says Dennis Rapp. "If they're not a team player, they don't stay here. Fortunately, we have a knowledgeable staff that has been with the company for many years."

For W.J. Rapp Company, Richmond has provided a stable environment with a diverse client base that the business fits into well. "We're a small enough business that we don't have to have rigid guidelines," says Rapp. "We can make adjustments to meet our clients' needs. And we're big enough and have the technology and equipment we need to handle the larger jobs and almost any job on short notice. We can make things happen."

W.J. RAPP COMPANY, INC. HAS BUILT A REPUTATION IN CENTRAL VIRGINIA FOR HIGH-QUALITY WORK, PEAK PERFORMANCE ON THE JOB, AND ETHICAL DEALINGS WITH CUSTOMERS.

James River Heating and Air Conditioning

N THE MORE THAN 30 YEARS THAT JAMES RIVER HEATING AND Air Conditioning has been in business, there have been major changes in the Richmond region; in the heating, ventilation, and air-conditioning business; and in the demands of the company's residential and commercial customers. But the company has adhered to the standards set by its founder, Hugh Joyce Sr., and, by following that track, it has continued to grow and prosper.

"We have a bunch of people here who really like what they do," says Hugh Joyce Jr., who succeeded his father as company president. "We have developed and are trying to maintain a culture that attracts and keeps great quality people. If we can keep them happy, they'll stay with us, and if they stay with us and continue to use their expertise, our customers will be happy. That's our formula for success."

Working With Hands, Heads, and Hearts

When Hugh Joyce Sr. founded James River in 1967, Richmond was just a suggestion of the city it is today, and the HVAC industry was just coming into its own. The business then focused on heating and air-conditioning, primarily in new construction. Today, the senior Joyce remains active in the business, which includes construction, service, design, and replacement in both residential and commercial facilities.

James River's primary service region is still Greater Richmond, but the company has expanded, purchasing Whitescarver Engineering Company, a Roanoke, Virginia-based commercial heating and air-conditioning service.

The business is divided into three operating groups: the residential service and replacement group, a commercial service and replacement group, and a commercial construction group. Hugh Joyce Jr. is the company president today, running the family-owned business that has grown into one of the largest HVAC service and installation operations in the region. But Joyce eagerly shares credit for the business' success.

James River has on staff more than 80 mechanics and technicians serving the marketplace from more than 100 trucks. The biggest difference between James River and the competition, however, is "the people we bring to do the work," Joyce says. They undergo continual training and work in a culture that encourages pride in a job well done.

Joyce recalls something he once read: A mechanic works with his hands, a technician with his head, and an artist with his hands, head, and his heart. "Our people are artists," he says. "When we come into someone's

HUGH JOYCE JR., PRESIDENT OF JAMES RIVER HEATING AND AIR CONDITIONING, RUNS A FAMILY-OWNED COMPANY THAT HAS BECOME ONE OF THE LARGEST OF ITS KIND IN THE GREATER RICHMOND REGION. THE COMPANY'S THREE OPERATING GROUPS HANDLE RESIDENTIAL AND COMMERCIAL HVAC SERVICE AND REPLACEMENT, AS WELL AS SYSTEM DESIGN AND INSTALLATION FOR NEW COMMERCIAL STRUCTURES.

house or business or factory, the customer will see that.

"One of our advantages is that many of the people who were here early in our history have grown with the firm, and today they hold many of the leadership positions at James River," he adds. Among those who have been with the firm from 25 to 30 years are David Norsworthy, senior vice president for commercial construction; Ruth East, vice president in charge of internal operations; and Leon Taylor, who heads commercial production. The first two technicians Hugh Joyce Sr. hired—Jack Thompson, head of the commercial service group, and Bruce Allsop, service manager—oversee about 50 technicians today.

Ready to Handle Large and Small Demands

James River's office, showroom, warehouse, and workshops are all under one roof on Westmoreland Street. The state-of-the-art production and service facility ranks as one of the finest HVAC facilities on the East Coast. There is even a satellite on the roof so company workers can monitor the weather in preparation for events that might affect customers.

The facility is located just off Broad Street, a major commercial thoroughfare near the center of the city. "We're proud of our business, and we want people to know who we are," Joyce says. He also points out that the location is within 15 minutes of almost any home or business in the region.

James River's customers come from a variety of places. The company works with more than 30,000 home-

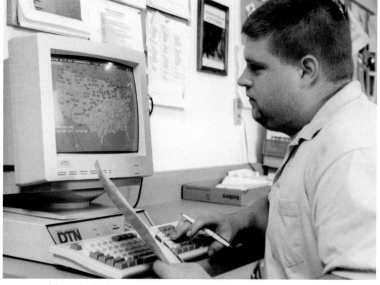

THE MORE THAN 80 MECHANICS AND TECHNICIANS WHO COMPRISE THE JAMES RIVER WORKFORCE UNDERGO CONTINUAL TRAINING AND WORK IN AN ENVIRONMENT THAT FOSTERS A JOB WELL DONE.

owners, although the largest segment of the business is the commercial service group. That group works with owner-occupied businesses, retail outfits, and industrial plant facilities. In this area, those clients include Ukrop's, SunTrust Bank, Arby's, Philip Morris, and The HON Company. "We will do a $50 project or a $2 million project," Joyce says. "We try to be responsive to what our clients need, which means we have to be flexible. We're able to go where the market is. That's been important to our longevity."

Comfortable in the Community

James River is not only about business. "We work equally as hard to give back to the community," Joyce says. The company won the Community Service Award for 2001—sponsored by Ukrop's and Commonwealth Catholic Charities—in recognition of its overall

volunteerism efforts. The company also has been named Small Business of the Year for Richmond and Virginia. "We are a bunch of Richmonders serving Richmonders and it shows," states Joyce.

Joyce describes James River as the ultimate high-tech company. It increasingly employs technology to solve customers' needs, using computers in all areas from design to service. The products and systems it installs are increasingly sophisticated, as are the "artists" who do the work. And customers are always demanding more from the heating, ventilation, and air-conditioning systems that operate in their facilities. "We can do it all. Ours is a one-call approach," Joyce says. "We provide design, functionality, and service, fit and finish, people and products, all coming together to keep people comfortable."

The Restaurant Company Inc.

WHEN RICHARD RIPP FOUNDED THE RESTAURANT COMPANY Inc. in 1967, he had already concluded that the new fast-food industry carried tremendous potential. Today, his company is widely recognized for innovations in building design, product quality, menu offerings, and service standards that set its restaurants apart from the competition. The public was quick to notice. ✦ The Restaurant Company's Arby's franchises surpassed Arby's restaurant sales locally and nationally. Its 18 Arby's franchised

restaurants in the Richmond metropolitan marketplace include four of the highest-sales restaurants in the entire Arby's system.

"The Restaurant Company's outstanding reputation among customers and within the Arby's system comes from absolutely delighting our customers with quality products, service, and experience that consistently exceed their expectations," says Vincent Ripp, Richard's son and the company's marketing director.

Success Based on Simple Principles

The Restaurant Company opened for business with about 25 employees and a menu that featured roast beef sandwiches, soft drinks, potato cakes, and milk shakes, including the signature Jamocha shake. Since then, The Restaurant Company has grown steadily to become a major employer in metropolitan Richmond, with more than 700 full-time and part-time workers, including people who work in areas such as architecture, research and development, marketing, and design.

The Restaurant Company's success is based on simple principles. The focus is on being friendlier, faster, more courteous, and quicker to recognize the customer's wants and needs. That improved focus means aggressively pursuing innovations that will achieve total customer satisfaction.

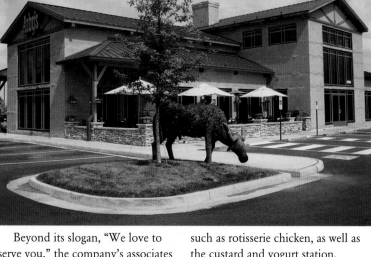

Beyond its slogan, "We love to serve you," the company's associates are actively involved in improving the business. Some work on the recruiting and retention committee, seeking to bring in and keep friendly, productive associates. Others are involved in community involvement programs, recipe monitoring, looking for ways to upgrade stores, and maintaining the satisfaction of their associates across the ranks.

The business has consistently been among Arby's leaders in innovation. With Richard Ripp frequently encouraging Arby's to expand its menu, the Richmond stores have introduced a variety of new products and concepts,

such as rotisserie chicken, as well as the custard and yogurt station.

The Restaurant Company also has pioneered new architectural styles, the most recent of which have raised the standards for the industry. These "super" Arby's restaurants resemble lodges, with tall ceilings, topiaries of steers and cowboys, high-back chairs, stone fireplaces, flat-screen televisions, and items that reflect western and northwestern themes.

Something for Every Taste

Today, the famous Arby's roast beef sandwiches continue to be the signature item on the menus. But these sandwiches have been joined by a

THE RUSTIC YET CONTEMPORARY ARCHITECTURE IS A STANDOUT IN THE SUBURBAN SURROUNDINGS OF SHORTPUMP.

A 30 FOOT SEE-THROUGH FIREPLACE WRAPPED IN STONE ANCHORS THE OPENNESS OF THE TIMBER TRUSS FRAMING PROVIDING A COZY EXPERIENCE ON THE DINING ROOM SIDE OF ARBY'S POUNCEY TRACT (LEFT).

THE CASUAL COMFORT OF A "LODGE" SETTING IS ENHANCED BY ANTIQUE CANOES, SUSPENDED CANADIAN GEESE SCULPTURES AND A TOTEM POLE CRAFTED BY NORTHWEST INDIAN CARVERS (RIGHT).

THE SERVING AREA COMBINES THE
ENERGY OF AN OPEN KITCHEN WITH
RICH GRANITE, MARBLE, AND MAHOGANY
APPOINTMENTS.

FRIENDLY ASSOCIATES SMILE AS THEY
AWAIT GUESTS AT ARBY'S TUCKERNUCK,
A WEST END LOCATION.

variety of other choices ranging from subs, market-fresh sandwiches, rotisserie chicken, fresh vegetable side dishes, potatoes, and an assortment of delicious chicken sandwiches. Diners can also make selections from a creative appetizer line called SideKickers or choose something from the Lite Menu.

The new super Arby's menus have expanded to include a Nito Burrito station with a variety of Mexican-American favorites; Pollo-Pronto, where customers can find slow-roasted chicken and turkey breasts that turn on a rotisserie before their eyes; and the Eskimo Pie Shoppe, which offers frozen custard and yogurt in cups, cones, sundaes, shakes, and concretes for dessert at the Colonial Heights location. The newest flagship in Short Pump, Virginia, offers Barbacoa, which sells barbecue made from beef brisket and smoked chicken; the Fresh Chef, serving made-to-order salads and stir-fry for more health conscious customers; and the Cool Blue station, offering refreshing fruity smoothies and fresh juices.

Creative Leadership and a Healthy Community

From the beginning, The Restaurant Company has reflected the energy, innovation, and vision of its founder. Richard Ripp's goal from the beginning has been to build a company that is among the most highly respected

food operators in the market. With a lean and productive upper management team that brings great depth of experience to the business, Ripp has reached that goal.

Leadership at the store level within the company also is strong and consistent, with many general managers having long tenures with the company. Turnover within The Restaurant Company is among the lowest in the industry. Top-notch training and orientation programs for new associates help them to maintain the company's high standards. At The Restaurant Company, service is—and always has been—the most important product.

Being active in the community has come naturally to The Restaurant Company. The firm is majority owner of the Richmond Kickers, a local professional soccer team. The com-

pany also sponsors WeatherNet on WWBT/NBC12. Through this program, local schools are provided with state-of-the-art weather stations where schoolchildren learn about meteorology and related subjects in science classes.

The Restaurant Company, Inc. seeks to surpass the $100 million sales figure by 2010, which will require continued hard work by its loyal, dedicated, and skilled staff. The company will open its first Fazoli's restaurant in 2002, and is looking for additional opportunities to expand.

"We have great passion and pride in what we do and what we can still accomplish," says Vincent Ripp. "Exceeding customer expectations, while benefiting company workers and the community, remains the primary goal of The Restaurant Company."

VIRGINIA COMMONWEALTH UNIVERSITY (VCU), ONE OF THE nation's most vibrant emerging research universities, has revitalized a large section of Richmond's city center, while contributing generously to the region's quality of life. With some 23,000 students engaged in a broad range of baccalaureate, master's, professional, doctoral, and postgraduate programs, VCU is unique among universities in Virginia. It has become an essential cornerstone on which the future of both the city and the state will be built.

Revival in the City

With an annual budget of more than $1 billion and a workforce of more than 15,500, VCU has grown remarkably since its establishment in 1968 by the Virginia General Assembly. The university is comprised of two campuses. Its 75-acre Academic Campus in Richmond's historic Fan District includes stately brownstones and modern structures built to complement old brick warehouses and industrial buildings nearby. Under President Eugene P. Trani, expansion of VCU's Academic Campus along Broad Street has brought new life to that prominent stretch of road. Two miles east, in the city's financial and government center, VCU's Medical College of Virginia (MCV) Campus includes MCV Hospitals—a center of world-class teaching, health care, and research.

Recent additions to the university include the Stuart C. Siegel Convocation and Recreation Center, a $29.7 million facility on Broad Street that has already proved popular for major events, retreats, and sports. The $35.7 million School of Engineering Building houses a clean room and other state-of-the-art facilities for students who will contribute to this highly technical, rapidly changing world. Both of these additions were built with substantial private contributions, which demonstrates the value the community places on VCU. The school's expansion also includes the new, $28 million Life Sciences Building, as well as the $13.8 million School of the Arts Building on the Academic Campus.

Building Academic Excellence

Now that VCU has taken command of its physical space, the university is redefining itself academically as well. The ultimate goals of this makeover are a greater emphasis on undergraduate education and the integration of undergraduate and graduate programs, as well as of business, government, and other professional interests in the area. Engineering, biotechnology, ethics and philosophy, the nationally recognized VCU Health System, and other disciplines and facilities are converging within the university's Life Sciences program, which will be the model for the integrated, cross-campus teaching approach.

With the city as a laboratory, VCU students work with the Science Museum of Virginia, Virginia Museum of Art, and Virginia Biotechnology Research Park, as well as with major high-tech companies in the area. The VCU Adcenter, with studios and classrooms in Shockoe Bottom—where its neighbors are among the nation's top ad agencies—has won national recognition. Several of VCU's traditional programs, such as social work, the arts, allied health, occupational and physical therapy, health administration, and design, continue to be among the best in the United States.

Already the most diverse university population in Virginia's highly regarded public higher education system, VCU is putting into place the people and facilities, the faculty and bench scientists, and the thinkers and technicians to build the future. The university has produced a steady stream of well-educated workers for new and old businesses. Striving to change the face of the city, Virginia Commonwealth University will be vital to Richmond well into the 21st century.

SOME 23,000 STUDENTS CHOOSE AMONG A BROAD RANGE OF DISCIPLINES OFFERED ON VIRGINIA COMMONWEALTH UNIVERSITY'S (VCU) TWO CAMPUSES.

IN 2000, VCU ATTRACTED NEARLY $120 MILLION IN RESEARCH FUNDING, A MAJORITY OF WHICH IS BASED ON VCU'S MEDICAL CAMPUS (LEFT).

VCU'S SCHOOL OF THE ARTS, WITH PROGRAMS RANGING FROM THEATER TO SCULPTURE, IS THE LARGEST PUBLIC ARTS SCHOOL IN THE UNITED STATES. THE SCHOOL'S SCULPTURE PROGRAM HAS BEEN HONORED AS ONE OF THE NATION'S BEST (RIGHT).

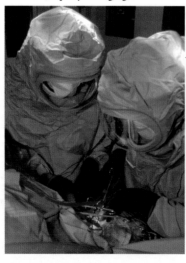

Colonial Mechanical Corporation

Oᴿɢᴀɴɪᴢᴇᴅ ᴀʀᴏᴜɴᴅ ʙᴏᴛʜ ᴀ ᴄᴏɴѕᴛʀᴜᴄᴛɪᴏɴ ᴀɴᴅ ᴀ ѕᴇʀᴠɪᴄᴇ group, Colonial Mechanical Corporation was founded in Richmond in 1972 by Bill McAllister. Specializing in preconstruction and design-build services, high-quality construction and installation, hands-on commissioning, preventive maintenance, and warranty and service repair, Colonial Mechanical today is one of the largest mechanical construction companies

in Virginia, ranking among the top 50 of such firms in the United States.

For more than 25 years, Colonial Mechanical has demonstrated leadership in customer service, technology, and vision in the field of construction and building services, ranging from small, special jobs to high-tech, high-end construction projects, to maintaining systems in office buildings and major industrial facilities. With single project value capabilities in excess of $20 million and a skilled workforce of more than 1,000, the company installs, maintains, and repairs all types of heating, ventilation, air-conditioning, plumbing, electrical, and process systems.

Colonial Mechanical sets out a threefold mission: providing superior mechanical construction and service to customers; recognizing and respecting employee contributions while providing for their security and career development; and ensuring the company's financial security while producing revenue to finance its growth.

"Leadership, integrity, professionalism, and commitment are what we are all about with our community, customers, and employees," says Mitch Haddon, service group president.

Uncompromising Dedication to Customer Satisfaction

The company's uncompromising dedication to customer satisfaction is supported by an outstanding inspection and quality assurance program. Colonial Mechanical provides continuous and consistent inspection, as well as review of fieldwork and in-house manufacturing, and relies on standardized quality control procedures that conform to—and often exceed—industry practices and local codes, as well as other applicable standards.

Colonial Mechanical's customers today include such central Virginia heavyweights as Infineon Technologies, DuPont, Philip Morris, Circuit City Stores, Ukrop's, Smurfit-Stone, Virginia BioTechnology Research Park, Federal Reserve Bank, Richmond Convention Center Authority, Capital One, and Bon Secours Hospitals.

Operating from a headquarters building off of Parham Road, Colonial Mechanical's manufacturing center includes one of the region's largest sheet metal and pipe fabrication facilities. The firm uses computer-aided design and drafting software in fabricating products, resulting in high-quality, fast-track delivery.

Known throughout the industry for its strong preconstruction abilities, Colonial Mechanical's engineering expertise has assisted many owners with budget and schedule problems before the ground is even broken.

Project superintendents have the authority to identify quality-related issues and to initiate solutions in the field. These skilled superintendents have the support of project managers, engineers, detailing and purchasing agents, and senior management. Fully documented checklists, inspections, and tests guarantee quality workmanship in the completed project.

Colonial Mechanical's orientation to safety is also evident in the extensive

CRYSTAL PHOTO, INC.

training its employees are given. The company employs full-time safety officers and implements incentive-based programs that further encourage safety. Colonial Mechanical conducts safety inspections at each work site to ensure that high-quality work is being performed in a timely, safe manner.

Extensive Resources Available to Customers

While Colonial Mechanical's expertise extends to related trades, the company handles mechanical needs, including equipment placements, renovations, short-duration construction projects, finish work, and design-build projects. The resources of the entire company are available to facilitate the special needs of each client. Where no mechanical or electrical drawings exist for a building, Colonial Mechanical can produce them. When conditions require on-site design and construction, the firm's managers and supervisors can do the job.

Webb Technologies is a more specialized business unit of Colonial Mechanical. While providing similar services in the Tidewater area, Webb also engineers and installs low-temperature refrigeration systems for cold storage distribution centers, manufacturing process systems, and medical facilities. Webb Technologies provides Colonial Mechanical with further depth by installing, maintaining, and repairing commercial and industrial refrigeration systems in the mid-Atlantic region.

Colonial Mechanical was acquired in 1998 by FirstEnergy Company, a diversified energy services company with more than $5 billion in annual revenues and assets, including 16 power plants nationwide. FirstEnergy provides Colonial Mechanical with access to emerging technologies, thus enhancing the company's ability to provide customers with energy-related solutions, as well as preparing the firm for changes that will take place in a deregulated marketplace.

Growing with the Community

Colonial encourages employees to participate in company decisions, including those related to the company's participation in the community. An employee citizenship committee determines how Colonial Mechanical will give back to the community through charitable contributions, which are funded by a percentage of the company's profits. Organizations like Richmond Children's Hospital and the Make-a-Wish Foundation have been among the many recipients of the firm's charitable efforts.

The company is also involved in apprenticeship programs that help train workers for the jobs of the future.

Colonial's growth has been consistent with Richmond's, with reference both to size and to sophistication. As the region has attracted new industries, Colonial Mechanical has raised the standards for its workers. "That has been a part of our growth process," Haddon says.

Richmond's location near the center of the state has proved advantageous, and Colonial Mechanical has furthered its presence outside the region with offices in northern Virginia, Roanoke, and Norfolk, the site of the firm's Webb business unit.

"Even with the tremendous growth in the Richmond area, business is still conducted with a focus on relationships based on hand-to-hand, face-to-face contact," Haddon says. "Our some 30 years of being in this community have allowed us to develop many partnerships, which have provided a foundation for growth and success. We consider ourselves very fortunate and are very grateful."

WITH SINGLE PROJECT VALUE CAPABILITIES IN EXCESS OF $20 MILLION AND A SKILLED WORKFORCE OF MORE THAN 1,000, THE COMPANY INSTALLS, MAINTAINS, AND REPAIRS ALL TYPES OF HEATING, VENTILATION, AIR-CONDITIONING, PLUMBING, ELECTRICAL, AND PROCESS SYSTEMS.

▲ CRYSTAL PHOTO, INC.

Ralph L. Samuels & Associates Inc.

A HOMEGROWN FIRM WHOSE ROOTS RUN DEEP, RALPH L. Samuels & Associates Inc. is committed to its clients, as well as to the community it has served for more than two decades. With some 20 licensed real estate agents working throughout the Richmond metropolitan area, the Samuels company has earned a reputation for putting buyers and sellers together in financial arrangements that benefit both parties.

And just as important as its financial success is the company's reputation for good citizenship. "Richmond is the only place I've ever lived, and I come from a large family that has grown with the town," says Ralph Samuels. "People know who we are, and we have developed a solid reputation for getting the job done. We cater to the customer. We always put the customer first."

Getting the Job Done

Samuels founded his business in 1974, originally as an insurance agency. By 1975, he had merged his business with the business of a lifelong friend who was already selling real estate. A few lucrative real estate investments later, Samuels decided to earn his real estate license, and by 1980, he had changed the company's name to reflect its role as a real estate agency.

Today, the Samuels firm specializes in residential real estate—while taking on some commercial projects—in the city of Richmond and its surrounding counties. The firm closes about 200 sales each year, many with repeat customers.

Samuels believes that operating a homegrown company means more than just doing business in a professional, honest manner; it also means involvement in community activities. The firm is an active sponsor of local events, including Youth Empowerment Day in the Highland Park Community, as well as Chimborazo Reunion in the Church Hill neighborhood where Samuels grew up.

As a result of this involvement, Samuels and the firm have earned commendations from various community groups, including a certificate of recognition from Richmond Public Schools for contributions to education and to students in the city, and a letter and proclamation from former Governor George Allen for community work. Samuels' firm also hosts an annual client appreciation dinner and dance during the Kwanza season.

"We are where we are because of our customers, and we want to show them that we appreciate it," Samuels says.

Improving the Quality of Work

Rather than having the company grow larger, Samuels hopes to continually improve the quality of work his people do. That means brokers and agents regularly update their knowledge of the market, financing, and technologies available to them.

"This is an organization that is community based, so our people have to do more than just a great job for their clients," Samuels says. "We want the kind of people who will be active in the community, in churches, and on boards and committees."

The agents of Ralph L. Samuels & Associates Inc. consider themselves as well prepared as any agents working anywhere for any company. "They are well educated in the sometimes complex world of financing, which is one of the critical aspects of any real estate deal, and they have solid contacts with lenders, so that they have the ability to complete any size deal," says Samuels. "This is our market. We know it. We have what it takes to get the job done."

"PEOPLE KNOW WHO WE ARE, AND WE HAVE DEVELOPED A SOLID REPUTATION FOR GETTING THE JOB DONE. WE CATER TO THE CUSTOMER. WE ALWAYS PUT THE CUSTOMER FIRST," SAYS RALPH L. SAMUELS (LEFT), PRINCIPAL BROKER OF RALPH L. SAMUELS & ASSOCIATES INC.

THE FIRM'S SALES PROMOTION CAMPAIGN, HOSTED IN CONJUNCTION WITH RYLAND HOMES, WAS A BIG SUCCESS (RIGHT).

Ŝ**INCE 1975, KBS, INC. HAS GROWN TO BECOME ONE OF THE** leading general contractors in the state of Virginia. The company has achieved this success by paying careful attention to its clients' needs and demands. KBS understands that successful long-term corporate partnerships begin with the relationships developed on each and every project. "We share a tremendous desire to satisfy the client and get the job done with

the highest quality," states Bill Paulette, founder and president. As evidence, KBS takes pride in the fact that more than half of the company's current projects represent repeat clients.

KBS is a vital contributor to Virginia's economic development. The contractor manages a variety of multimillion-dollar projects, ranging from office buildings and retail sites to assisted living facilities, hotels, and apartments. The company's construction portfolio also includes museums, entertainment complexes, and industrial facilities, as well as historic renovations. In 2000, the silver anniversary of KBS, the company topped $120 million in construction projects. "We're committed to many, many years of success," Paulette vows. "We're growing every day, and that helps make Richmond a dynamic place to live and work."

A Family Approach to Business

KBS takes pride in achievements that can be attributed in part to its family business approach. The KBS family includes Paulette and his longtime collaborators, Vice Presidents Dennis Lynch and Bill Loughridge. By encouraging and supporting skilled workers—many of whom have been with the company since its inception—KBS has achieved a record of dependability, superior work, and consistency. The same enduring relationships are found among KBS' subcontractors, including many of the region's finest craftsmen and tradesmen, who were instrumental to KBS' success when the company began and still work with the firm today.

As KBS has grown, the company has continued to recruit the best in the business—individuals whose skills were honed managing and building some of the most complex facilities in the United States.

Work That Builds Community

KBS is proud to have worked on many of Richmond's schools and public buildings. One of the community's most prized projects is the $13 million renovation of the historic Maggie L. Walker High School, which will house the Governor's School for Government and International Studies. The renovation work will create a technology-rich environment, while preserving the historical integrity of the school. KBS orchestrated a similar transformation in Petersburg, in the renovation of the old Petersburg High School. Today, that building is home to the Appomattox Regional Governor's School.

KBS has been involved in high-profile work at some of the region's landmark buildings, including the Library of Virginia State Records Facility and the Science Museum of Virginia. Along with the restoration and preservation of some of Richmond's historic past, KBS has also been building with an eye on Richmond's future.

To serve the needs of the local community, the company has built apartments, office buildings, and shopping centers. KBS is equally proud to be working with local retailers, like Ukrop's Super Markets, and being entrusted to build national anchor stores such as Sears and Lowe's Home Improvement Centers.

In addition, KBS has been an active member of the Richmond Chapter of the Associated General Contractors (AGC) of Virginia. The AGC is involved with local and statewide legislation, educational programs, and community outreach projects such as the Christmas in April program, which assists the elderly and disabled of Richmond with sorely needed home repairs.

KBS has been a proud sponsor of an innovative middle school program created by the National Association of Women in Construction. This outreach initiative provides a yearlong curriculum that introduces students to career opportunities in the construction industry. KBS enjoys being involved in local community programming, and is pleased to be associated with educational efforts directed at the future of the central Virginia area.

As the 21st century unfolds, KBS, Inc. has built a foundation of solid partnerships and stands ready to contribute to the economic progress of Virginia.

S**INCE 2000, KBS, INC. HAS OPERATED THROUGH THREE PRIMARY LINES OF BUSINESS, WHICH SERVE AS UMBRELLAS FOR THE DIVERSE TYPES OF PROJECTS FOR WHICH THE GENERAL CONTRACTOR IS KNOWN. THE RETAIL LINE INCLUDES THE COMPANY'S WORK IN BOTH STAND-ALONE AND MAJOR SHOPPING CENTERS, INCLUDING THE CONSTRUCTION OF MALL ANCHOR STORES. IN ADDITION TO HANDLING TRADITIONAL OFFICE-BUILDING CONSTRUCTION, THE INSTITUTIONAL AND COMMERCIAL DIVISION IS RESPONSIBLE FOR KBS' WORK IN MUSEUM AND SCHOOL CONSTRUCTION. THE MULTIFAMILY, ASSISTED LIVING, AND HOTELS DIVISION INCLUDES KBS' GROWING VOLUME OF APARTMENT COMPLEXES, AS WELL AS ASSISTED LIVING FACILITIES AND PROJECTS IN THE HOSPITALITY INDUSTRY. MANAGEMENT OF KBS INCLUDES (FROM LEFT) DENNIS LYNCH, BILL LOUGHRIDGE, RICH LEE, AND BILL PAULETTE.**

Crews & Hancock P.L.C.

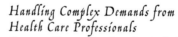

SINCE ITS FOUNDING IN 1975, CREWS & HANCOCK P.L.C. has established itself as one of the nation's leading law firms with expertise in health and insurance law. As the firm has grown, it has expanded its focus to include the wide range of legal services that its clients demand. Stated succinctly, Crews & Hancock offers "innovative legal solutions for your health care, business, and insurance needs." With some 80

employees, including more than 40 lawyers, the firm is not so large that clients get less than the most careful, personal attention. By maintaining its focus on health and hospital law, insurance law, litigation, and general corporate law, the firm is capable of offering all of the expertise of a large firm. It does so for more than 1,500 clients nationwide from its headquarters in Richmond's Main Street financial district and its offices in Fairfax, Roanoke, and Virginia Beach.

Seeing a Need and Filling It

John William Crews and Thomas F. Hancock III had represented numerous health-related agencies as assistant attorneys general for Virginia by the time they founded the firm. Through their work, they had come to see the need for skilled attorneys in health and hospital law and related fields, and set out to fill that need. More than 25 years later, Crews & Hancock offers a wide range of legal services on virtually all laws pertaining to the health care industry.

As the firm developed this expertise, it expanded its services to areas such as risk management, employment law, and health care compliance. This broader capacity enables the firm to

FROM LEFT: THOMAS F. HANCOCK III AND JOHN WILLIAM CREWS

offer comprehensive legal assistance to the health care organizations and other interests that make up its list of clients. Today, Crews & Hancock stands out as Virginia's only law firm with a primary emphasis on health and hospital law.

Handling Complex Demands from Health Care Professionals

Crews & Hancock's client list includes health care trade associations, health systems, hospitals, insurance companies, HMOs, nursing homes, assisted living facilities, pharmaceutical companies, psychiatric and substance abuse centers, physicians, and a broad range of other professionals and professional corporations.

The variety of legal services Crews & Hancock offers reflects the growing complexity of the health care industry. Experience has shown that teams organized into specialty areas best address client needs. These include corporate law, insurance law, administrative law, risk management, corporate security and safety, employment practices, civil litigation, appellate practice, and legislative services.

For more than 20 years, the firm has served as general counsel to a leading professional liability insurance carrier. It has also represented reciprocal insurers, risk retention groups, risk purchasing groups, captive insurance companies, self-insuring associations, and insurance and risk financing entities throughout the United States.

While the firm's litigation team has successfully handled a full range of cases, the firm also specializes in helping clients minimize risks. Lawyers are available after hours with

INSURANCE LAW TEAM: JOHN B. MUMFORD, MATTHEW A. HADDAD, KATHERINE BENSON BAIN, FRANK J. RUSSO III, SCOTT J. SORKIN; (BOTTOM ROW) MARTHA L. STEELE, JOHN W. "BILL" CREWS, RICHARD W.E. BLAND

instantaneous advice, should a potential problem emerge. This often means focusing not so much on the legal issues as on the emotional trauma health care providers must face. The Crews & Hancock approach is to strive to make sure communication is maintained between the provider and the patient or the patient's family both in good times and when untoward events arise. The goal is to head off lawsuits that often result from poor communications.

Expanding to Meet Growing Demands of Clients

Crews & Hancock also has a record of success in helping clients with issues in the growing specialties of corporate security and safety. This can mean taking a more proactive approach to such concerns as internal investigations, employee privacy, workplace safety, employee screening, and the regulatory environment. The firm offers expertise in a variety of labor- and employment-related fields such as policy development, educational programs, and the best approaches to hiring and discharging employees. All of these steps can help businesses avoid any potential problems that may arise.

Crews & Hancock also is a capable advocate for clients who go before governmental entities, with more than 25 years' experience before the Virginia General Assembly on matters including tort reform, medical malpractice litigation, wetlands protection, business organization structures, and title protection for professionals.

Commitment to Quality Legal Services

The key to Crews & Hancock's continued success will be its people, who have established a firm culture based on commitment to quality legal services, personal service, and cost-effective legal representation. This commitment and the collegial atmosphere at the firm enable it to attract talented law school graduates and seasoned attorneys.

The firm uses a team approach to most problems. Clients receive all of the services they need from trial lawyers, legal assistants, the firm's principals, and attorneys within the firm whose expertise may be needed in any specific situation. This produces timely, innovative, and valuable solutions for clients. And the firm's appellate team has a substantial record of success with appeals to forums including the Virginia Supreme Court, the

Fourth U.S. Circuit Court of Appeals, and the U.S. Supreme Court.

Crews & Hancock also supports various continuing education and community-minded activities. Its attorneys serve as faculty for Virginia State Bar and health care-related continuing education seminars, and are published regularly in client and legal publications. They are highly regarded in areas such as medical malpractice, peer review, preemployment screening, patient dumping, workplace violence, and Medicare and Medicaid reimbursement issues. Some of the firm's lawyers also serve on boards for nonprofit and charitable organizations.

It is this combination of expertise, organization, and intangibles that Crews & Hancock P.L.C.'s people bring that has been and will continue to be at the heart of the firm's successful representation of its clients.

CLOCKWISE FROM TOP LEFT: CORPORATE LAW TEAM: WILLIAM H. HALL JR., WILLIAM O. QUIREY JR., MARY C. MALONE, B. PAGE GRAVELY JR., STEPHANIE L. HISS, JEANNIE A. ADAMS, JAMES M. DANIEL JR., PATRICK F. HEINEN; (BOTTOM ROW) MARTIN A. DONLAN JR., THOMAS F. HANCOCK III, PETER M. MELLETTE. NOT PICTURED: THOMAS T. PALMER, L. THOMPSON HANES

LITIGATION TEAM (RICHMOND OFFICE): MARK H. SCHMIDT, JOHN R. REDMOND, W. SCOTT JOHNSON, JAMES J. ILIJEVICH, WIRT P. MARKS IV, SEAN P. BYRNE; (BOTTOM ROW) JUDITH B. HENRY, KAREN A. GOULD, ANGELA C. FLEMING. NOT PICTURED: WESLEY G. RUSSELL JR.

LITIGATION TEAM (FAIRFAX OFFICE): COLLEEN GENTILE, GEORGE O. PETERSON, CHRISTINA S. YEHLE, MICHAEL E. OLSZEWSKI, KATHERINE R. MCMILLEN; (BOTTOM ROW) RICHARD L. NAGLE, THOMAS L. APPLER, JOHN E. MCINTOSH JR.

FOR UPSCALE SHOPPING IN CENTRAL VIRGINIA, WISE SHOPPERS go directly to Regency Square. There, in a comfortable, attractive setting, they find an unmatched mix of retailers and services. Since 1975, Regency has been home to top department stores, as well as a unique selection of individual and local retailers. Alongside this fabulous shopping, Regency offers consumers a wide variety of amenities—through Regency

Services at the Concierge Desk—and a great selection of casual dining choices to suit many tastes.

A Center for the Community

In 2000, Regency Square celebrated 25 years as one of the area's favorite places for shopping, special events, and holiday celebrations. The premier shopping destination is as inviting today as it was the day it opened, with its bubbling fountains, sculptured art forms, indoor gardens, and classic marble-and-glass ambience. Patrons of the mall also appreciate Regency's well-lit parking areas, which include two covered parking lots.

Located in Richmond's fashionable, affluent West End, Regency Square is easily accessible from all regions. Regency's central location places it only 15 minutes from downtown, 20 minutes from Richmond International Airport, and less than an hour from Charlottesville and Williamsburg. It is just minutes from some of the region's preferred hotels and motels, restaurants, theaters, museums, and other attractions, so a few days in Richmond can

easily include a visit to this unique shopping destination, which boasts some of the largest, most popular department stores in the region. Regency is home to Hecht's flagship store, JCPenney, and Sears, Roebuck and Co.

Altogether, the mall is home to more than 100 stores, including such popular, high-quality national retailers as Eddie Bauer, Abercrombie & Fitch, Gap, Banana Republic, J. Crew, Brooks Brothers, Caché, Godiva Chocolatier, Sephora, and Williams-Sonoma. More

than one-third of its stores are specialty shops that no other area mall has.

Together, the shops at Regency are filled with women's, men's, and children's apparel; shoes; jewelry; books; cards; gifts; toys; music; electronics; home accessories; and hard-to-find specialty items. Still other stores feature bath, beauty, and health products and services; hair stylists; banking services; and nationally known providers of auto services and products.

SINCE 1975, REGENCY SQUARE HAS BEEN HOME TO TOP DEPARTMENT STORES, AS WELL AS A UNIQUE SELECTION OF NATIONAL AND LOCAL RETAILERS.

Providing Shoppers What They Want

Regency Square knows from research that shoppers want to save time and money. So, the center created an E-mail bulletin where the customer receives a concise, weekly update of sales, special promotions, new merchandise arrivals, and downloadable coupons for their choice of stores. The center's Web site, www.shopregencysqmall.com, also features a pictorial gift guide section that is keyed to specific ages, interests, seasons, and price ranges. Plus, the site's convenient gift reminder service means never forgetting another special occasion. Anyone can register birthdays and other important gift-giving dates on the site, which then generates an automatic E-mail reminder when the event nears.

And, for busy shoppers in need of a break, Regency offers a good selection of eateries in a pleasant setting. There are individual dining choices in the convenient food court, as well as a popular full-service restaurant at the mall. Regency Square features Regency Services at the Concierge Desk to provide superior customer service and amenities that are unusual for a shopping mall.

Customers find that convenient items like shopping bags, strollers, and wheelchairs are available at Regency Services. And in one stop at the mall, shoppers can pick up stamps, send a fax, and take advantage of copying services. Gift boxing is not just a sea-sonal service, as Regency customers can have gifts wrapped and boxed year-round.

For holidays, birthdays, or any special occasion, a Regency Square gift certificate is always the perfect gift. Gift certificates are attractively boxed and can be redeemed at any store throughout the mall.

A center for community life that extends far beyond shopping, Regency Square is constantly contributing to the region's economic and cultural well-being. Regency Square often hosts school and community groups for a variety of special events, and recently supported organizations such as Dress for Success, Breast Cancer Foundation, Henrico County Schools, and Children's Miracle Network.

LOCATED JUST 15 MINUTES FROM DOWNTOWN RICHMOND, MORE THAN A THIRD OF REGENCY SQUARE'S STORES ARE SPECIALTY SHOPS, HELPING MAKE IT THE CITY'S PREMIER SHOPPING DESTINATION.

SINCE IT OPENED MORE THAN A QUARTER CENTURY AGO, Westminster-Canterbury Richmond has earned national recognition, community support, and the loyalty of its residents and their families. Rated by *New Choices* magazine as one of the 20 best continuing care retirement communities in the nation, Westminster-Canterbury provides a financially sound, vibrant community that is home to some 600 people.

This unusual joint venture of local Presbyterian and Episcopal denominations opened in 1975. Westminster-Canterbury's mission as a faith-based organization has been to deliver services that are specific to each resident's needs in a professional, compassionate, holistic manner. The company extends that mission to its employees, seeking to provide a meaningful working environment. Westminster-Canterbury also extends its resources through dynamic leadership in the community.

LIBBY CLARK

RATED BY *New Choices* MAGAZINE AS ONE OF THE 20 BEST CONTINUING CARE RETIREMENT COMMUNITIES IN THE NATION, WESTMINSTER-CANTERBURY PROVIDES A FINANCIALLY SOUND, VIBRANT COMMUNITY THAT IS HOME TO SOME 600 PEOPLE.

A Place for Living Enriched, Fulfilling Lives

Life at Westminster-Canterbury can be as intellectually, spiritually, and physically stimulating as anything residents have ever experienced. The full-service community provides services ranging from independent living to skilled nursing care. Westminster-Canterbury's capable management and strong financial position provide residents and their families with the peace of mind that comes from knowing there is a place for them, no matter what needs may arise.

As the number of seniors in the overall population continues to grow, so has the demand for retirement communities such as Westminster-Canterbury to provide a wide range of stimulating activities that will enhance residents' lives. At Westminster-Canterbury, that can mean viewing the extensive art collection, swimming in the indoor pool, browsing through shops, or taking classes in everything from ballroom dancing to painting and conversational Spanish to computing. There are concerts, exercise classes, and historical and architectural tours as well. Westminster-Canterbury also offers a regular program of outstanding events, such as book-and-author dinners, concerts, lectures, and other programs through the community's Cultural and Educational Series.

LIBBY CLARK

CHUCK SAVAGE

Though Westminster-Canterbury is affiliated with the Presbyterian and Episcopal churches, religious activities are ecumenical in scope. Residents represent more than 120 different faith groups, a combination that makes for a rich spiritual mix.

A Place for Every Lifestyle and Need

Westminster-Canterbury residents enjoy a number of attractive lifestyle options. There are studios, one- or two-bedroom apartments, and cottages with up to 3,000 square feet of living space. Independent living represents an active lifestyle where residents choose from the 26 floor plans designed to fit every taste and pocketbook.

Westminster-Canterbury's Garden apartments, which opened in 1995, offer spacious designs with terraces or balconies. The Glebe is a neighborhood of freestanding homes near the main building. These homes feature private yards, gardens, decks, fireplaces, garages, and hardwood floors.

As part of Westminster-Canterbury's continuum of services, Morningside, the Pavilion, and the Suite create intermediate steps between independent living accommodations and nursing services. An experienced staff provides support services as needed by the

residents in these assisted living, all-private apartments.

No matter where the resident at Westminster-Canterbury resides, there is an attractive dining room nearby. Residents select from a varied and healthy menu that is created by experienced chefs and served in a sociable, attractive environment.

A Model for Retirement Communities

Westminster-Canterbury's reputation for excellence has been accompanied by a high occupancy rate and an extensive waiting list. To provide the services today's residents expect, Westminster-Canterbury relies on a staff of some 640 employees, including more than 100 certified nursing assistants. These employees, many of whom have been at Westminster-Canterbury for more than a decade, prepare and serve meals, clean apartments and maintain grounds, provide recreational and spiritual enrichment, and personalize all services provided to residents.

A model for several other retirement communities in Virginia, Westminster-Canterbury, since its opening, has provided homes for thousands of older adults, as well as thousands of jobs that enrich the

Richmond region's economy. Its impressive financial strength has earned Westminster-Canterbury a Standard & Poor's A bond rating, the first given to a continuing care community in Virginia. It also was the first retirement community in Richmond to meet the strict standards of excellence of the Continuing Care Accreditation Commission.

Members of Westminster-Canterbury's staff have been elected leaders within the American Association of Nonprofit Homes for the Aging, and are in demand as speakers at the association's conferences and meetings.

Hundreds of faithful donors and talented volunteer leaders of the Westminster-Canterbury Foundation make possible a strong financial aid program. This Fellowship Program provides grants of more than $2 million annually to residents who, without such help, could not live at Westminster-Canterbury. The foundation's strong endowment continues to grow, securing the lives of current and future residents. The foundation helps Westminster-Canterbury honor its commitment that no resident will ever have to leave the community because of financial problems. The program helps more than 12 percent of all residents with the costs of home and health care.

Westminster-Canterbury Richmond's future was secured in 2000 with the purchase of 25 acres adjacent to the original campus. With this acquisition come plans for expanded services that will continue to set new standards for the industry. A master plan for the entire 50-acre campus will allow Westminster-Canterbury to continue to be the constantly evolving community that has marked its 25-year-plus history.

AT WESTMINSTER-CANTERBURY ACTIVITIES CAN INCLUDE VIEWING THE EXTENSIVE ART COLLECTION, SWIMMING IN THE INDOOR POOL, BROWSING THROUGH SHOPS, OR TAKING CLASSES IN EVERYTHING FROM BALLROOM DANCING TO PAINTING AND CONVERSATIONAL SPANISH TO COMPUTING. THERE ARE CONCERTS, EXERCISE CLASSES, AND HISTORICAL AND ARCHITECTURAL TOURS AS WELL.

Woodfin Oil

FROM ITS FAMILIAR ADS FEATURING BARKING GERMAN shepherds to its fleet of red-white-and-blue trucks, Woodfin Oil has established a comfortable presence in Richmond—like the commercials say—as "Your number one faithful friend." And comfort is a reason this homegrown company has risen to the top in a competitive marketplace. "We are the best at what we do," says Jack Woodfin, vice president and son of

the company's founder. Thousands of Richmond-area residents call on the Woodfin company, with its service technicians and quality products, to stay warm in the winter and cool in the summer. And that is the way it has been for some 25 years.

Beginning with an Opportunity
John H. Woodfin Sr. started Woodfin Oil in 1977, after working more than

13 years in the oil business. The opportunity to come home to Richmond and buy Exxon's home heating oil business was something he could not resist. And the results have been all Woodfin could have imagined.

Today, Woodfin Oil is one of the area's largest home heating oil businesses, with more than 300 employees and three main offices. The company's headquarters is in Mechanicsville, north

of the city. The firm maintains key locations on Stockton Street south of the James River and near oil terminals, as well as on Ellen Road in the industrial area near the Diamond. It also has offices in Goochland and King William counties, and has moved into the Fredericksburg market as well.

And with computerization and the high-tech heating and air-conditioning systems Woodfin Oil installs and maintains, the company is growing rapidly with the community.

Branching Out and Building on Its Foundation
Beginning in the 1980s, Woodfin branched out into new areas with its WATCHCARD and Pit Stop operations. WATCHCARD is a commercial fuel business with about 30 fleet refueling stations conveniently located for customers from Tidewater to Charlottesville. WATCHCARD provides diesel fuel and gasoline to businesses that run fleets of vehicles.

Under the Pit Stop brand, the company owns approximately 15 service stations, some of which contain

FROM ITS FAMILIAR ADS FEATURING BARKING GERMAN SHEPHERDS TO ITS FLEET OF RED-WHITE-AND-BLUE TRUCKS, WOODFIN OIL HAS ESTABLISHED A COMFORTABLE PRESENCE IN RICHMOND— LIKE THE COMMERCIALS SAY—AS "YOUR NUMBER ONE FAITHFUL FRIEND."

BEGINNING IN THE 1980S, WOODFIN BRANCHED OUT INTO NEW AREAS WITH ITS WATCHCARD AND PIT STOP OPERATIONS.

sandwich shops, doughnut shops, and mini-markets. These stations can be found as far east as Williamsburg, as far north as Fredericksburg, and as far west as Lexington, Virginia.

Still, the residential heating and air-conditioning business is Woodfin's biggest, highest-profile business. The secret to Woodfin's success in this area has been simple: "We will do it better than anybody else to keep our customers comfortable and happy," Jack Woodfin says. "That means sending out the best technicians on the East Coast to do heating and cooling installation and service. And it means providing the best products, whether you're talking about heating oil or an air-conditioning system. We do what's best for each customer's needs."

New Technology Keeps Woodfin Out Front

As in many fields, technological advances have changed the heating oil business over the last decade, and Woodfin has taken full advantage of those advances. Today, oil burners are the most efficient system available for home heating needs, according to Woodfin, with some reaching 90 percent efficiency, compared with just

30 percent for some electric systems. "That shows what technology has done in that area," Woodfin says. And the computer revolution also has had an impact on the company's ability to meet customer needs quickly and efficiently. The company's computer system, along with outstanding technicians and top-quality products, creates Woodfin's focus: customer-first, quality service.

In recent years, Woodfin's service vehicles have been equipped with the Pegasus on-board computer system, which is similar to systems used by UPS and FedEx. Through this computerized system, Woodfin can tell customers almost precisely when a technician will be at their house for a service call—enabling customers to use their time more efficiently, since they can avoid the unpleasant waiting game that is necessary with many services.

"We know the customer's time is as valuable as ours," Woodfin says. "This careful scheduling is something our customers can count on. We all consider it a real plus."

The company's computer system is more than just a convenience. Woodfin says the firm's fleet of technicians usually work in specific

areas so they will become familiar with individual customers and their heating and air-conditioning systems. Often, the same technician installs the system and checks on it later if the customer has questions.

But in emergencies or in busy times, that particular technician is not always available. "With the computer, we can give the technician all of the customer's information so he's an expert on the home's system," Woodfin says. "He probably can go right to the problem, which saves him time and the customer money. Nobody else in this market has this capability."

For the Woodfins, Richmond was a place to come home to in 1977, and it remains a comfortable fit for the business. "We have grown along with the residential and commercial growth here," Jack Woodfin says. "It's been steady. The kind of workers we've been able to hire are people who work hard and are loyal to the business and the customers. That's an advantage you won't find in a lot of places.

"We're the heating oil dealer of choice in town, and people recognize that," adds Woodfin. "We can meet all those needs, winter or summer. We run hot and cold."

1980 Waste Management, Inc.

1983 William Henry Harris & Associates Inc.

1984 CIGNA HealthCare of Virginia, Inc.

1984 Eagle Construction of Virginia, Inc.

1984 Richmond Marriott

1988 The Berkeley Hotel

1988 Holiday Inn Select-Koger Conference Center

1989 Open Plan Systems

1990 Halifax Corporation

1990 Mexico Restaurant

1992 Community Pride

1995 Brooks Building Company

1996 Infineon Technologies Richmond

1997 Freedom Inc. Home Health

1997 Networking Technologies and Support Inc.

1998 Wachovia Bank, N.A.

1999 The Grove Swift Creek

Waste Management, Inc.

WITH A CLEAR, CONSISTENT FOCUS ON THE FUNDAMENTAL values of trust, service, and commitment, Waste Management, Inc. has earned a place in the Richmond community and across Virginia as a valued corporate citizen. Since 1980, the company has provided good jobs, substantial revenue, and environmentally sensitive solutions to the waste disposal needs of the communities it serves. ❧ "Serving Virginia's citizens and protecting the environment are imperative to our success," says Robert Kania, region vice president. "Whether through the professionalism of our employees, the financial commitment to our host communities, or our community involvement, we are dedicated to ensuring a stronger, cleaner Virginia for all citizens."

Investing in Virginia with Jobs, Operations

One of the largest providers of waste management services in the world, Waste Management operates 21 facilities–from hauling companies to landfills–in Virginia. To date, the company has invested more than $450 million in building and upgrading these facilities, which handle materials ranging from household garbage to construction debris.

Waste Management's landfills are a significant source of revenue to their communities. In 2000, the company contributed more than $14.4 million to Virginia localities through various business license fees, property taxes, and goods and services purchased. Additionally, Waste Management pays each community hosting a landfill a fee for each ton deposited in its landfill. These host fees are often used to provide municipal services, build schools, and reduce local taxes.

Waste Management provides jobs for more than 1,000 citizens of Virginia and has an annual payroll in excess of $38 million. The company makes it a priority to purchase goods and services in Virginia whenever possible. The economic impact of these local purchases has, to date, amounted to more than $80 million.

Reaching Out to Host Communities

The impact of Waste Management extends far beyond the tax assessor's office. In its host communities, the company often provides services either at a reduced cost or at no cost. In 1999, these contributions amounted to more than $5.4 million. These valuable services extend beyond curbside trash pickup and recycling programs. The company also provides most host communities with fully manned convenience centers where county residents can dispose of their solid waste.

Waste Management's employees live and work in their host communities and are active in various organizations such as schools, Rotary Club, and local charities. They also work with environmental groups, in archaeological explorations, and in neighborhood cleanups. With financial contributions topping $95,000 in 1999, the company supports museums, the Special Olympics, chambers of commerce, and volunteer rescue squads as well.

Education is a prime focus of Waste Management's community involvement. At its Middle Peninsula Landfill in Gloucester, Virginia, the company has an environmental scientist on staff as a business and education coordinator. His work with schools and other community organizations has promoted recycling throughout the community.

Says Kania, "These are men and women who are involved in the community and care about the environment, their neighborhood, and their neighbors." Waste Management's primary goal is to provide a clean and safe environment for Virginia and its future generations.

WASTE MANAGEMENT, INC.'S PRIMARY GOAL IS TO PROVIDE A CLEAN AND SAFE ENVIRONMENT FOR VIRGINIA AND ITS FUTURE GENERATIONS.

AT A TIME WHEN HEALTH CARE BENEFITS ARE BECOMING MORE and more complicated, and when both consumers and employers have less and less time to deal with them, CIGNA HealthCare of Virginia, Inc. offers a simple solution. "Our goal is to make sure that our members get the care they need when they need it," says Nicholas Gettas, M.D., medical director. ≈ "By providing convenient access to quality health care, simple

and easy-to-use administration, hassle-free service, access to useful information, and predictable costs, we return value to people's lives," says Gettas. "In doing so, we make our customers' lives simpler and easier—improving their health, well-being, financial security, and peace of mind, all at an affordable and predictable price."

Putting National Expertise to Work in Richmond

The CIGNA HealthCare companies comprise one of the nation's leading providers of health benefit programs, with managed care and indemnity products marketed in all 50 states and managed care networks serving 45 states, the District of Columbia, and Puerto Rico.

CIGNA HealthCare of Virginia, Inc. has been serving the needs of central and southeastern Virginians in the Richmond and Hampton Roads areas since 1984. With more than 300,000 members in the company's health benefit plans, CIGNA HealthCare of Virginia offers one of the largest health networks in the Commonwealth.

"We have a special understanding of the needs of the residents of Virginia," says Greg Bowman, president and general manager. "Our members appreciate that CIGNA HealthCare of Virginia is locally driven and locally managed. Most of our decisions are made right here in Richmond at our office in the Boulders."

Helping Consumers Better Manage Their Health

CIGNA HealthCare of Virginia is helping its members to have access to the right care, from the right provider, in the right setting, at the right time. Through an extensive portfolio of managed care and indemnity medical, dental, and pharmacy plans, CIGNA HealthCare offers its members a broad spectrum of health and wellness services to meet individual health needs.

Preventive Care Services includes regular checkups, immunizations, and screening tests for men, women, and children. The CIGNA HealthCare 24-Hour Health Information Line℠, CIGNA HealthCare *Well-Being* newsletter, and an interactive Web site are just a sampling of the special programs available.

The CIGNA HealthCare Well Aware Program for Better Health® offers individualized support and educational materials for members with chronic medical conditions such as asthma, diabetes, and low back pain. The program is designed to help plan members manage their condition, make daily self-care easier, and encourage a more effective interaction with the member's physician.

Committed to Quality, Committed to Community

CIGNA HealthCare of Virginia demonstrates its commitment to quality every day in all aspects of its business. The company continually measures progress toward achieving quality goals, and introduces new ways to give plan members the medical coverage and service quality they expect. The National Committee for Quality Assurance (NCQA), an independent, not-for-profit organization that evaluates managed care plans, has awarded

CIGNA HealthCare of Virginia, Inc. a Commendable accreditation.

CIGNA HealthCare of Virginia supports many national and local initiatives and organizations, including the March of Dimes, National Multiple Sclerosis Society, American Heart Association, and Shots for Tots, as well as Virginia Breast Cancer Awareness Month.

Today, CIGNA HealthCare of Virginia, Inc. is a shining example of a firm that is dedicated not just to the bottom line, but also to the people it serves. With that philosophy firmly in place, the company will continue to be a thriving member of the Richmond community for decades to come.

GREG BOWMAN, PRESIDENT OF CIGNA HEALTHCARE OF VIRGINIA, INC., WAS THE CHAIRMAN FOR THE MARCH OF DIMES WALK AMERICA IN RICHMOND.

LEFT TO RIGHT: CHRIS HAASE, LEE HANNAH, AND CHRIS LEAHY DISCUSS A CLIENT'S RENEWAL.

William Henry Harris & Associates Inc.

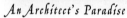

In the 20 years that William Henry "Harry" Harris III has worked as an architect, he has become one of the busiest and most successful designers of church facilities and buildings for religious organizations in the region. With more than $20 million of work under construction, William Henry Harris & Associates Inc. provides clients with services that include master planning, feasibility studies, renovation, historic preservation design, and architectural design.

"We know that people are putting a lot of trust into what we do," Harris says. "We take this work seriously, and we really enjoy doing it."

Firm History

After graduating from the University of Virginia, Harris spent several years working with some of Virginia's top architectural firms. In 1983, he decided the time had come to set out on his own. Initially, his work consisted mostly of residential projects and, for Harris, who enjoys sailing, designing waterfront homes around Virginia's Northern Neck and Middle Peninsula.

One day, members of a church approached him about a project that another architect had undertaken and been unable to finish. Harris took over the job, and he was on his way.

"They liked what I did, and someone recommended me to another church. Before I knew it, we had designed several church buildings in the area. We've been busy ever since." These days, Harris says, he gets two or three calls a week from church leaders asking about projects they would like to have built.

An Architect's Paradise

A Richmond native whose roots in the city run more than a century deep, Harris moved his practice to its current offices among historic and architecturally significant structures in 1987. This central location allows Harris to appreciate his surroundings. "From the standpoint of being in Richmond, this is a great place. Walk down this street and look close, and you'll see some beautiful work, beautiful buildings. For an architect, it's like being in paradise."

Harris's firm includes four licensed architects and several support personnel, focusing primarily on the religious community in central Virginia, the Northern Neck, and the Middle Peninsula. Most of the work includes additions to existing church buildings. From time to time, however, Harris will design an entirely new campus for a church. Recent commissions include a $9 million addition to the Second Baptist Church in Richmond's West End.

The firm also has worked at schools and courthouses, as well as on other projects. Among its more significant contributions has been the master plan and new Lower School Building at St. Christopher's School, a private school in Richmond.

Harris also takes pride in his pro bono work with Elk Hill Farm, the site of a residential program for young men. A board member for 20 years, Harris laid out the campus and designed numerous buildings for the farm, including a dining hall, gymnasium, dormitories, an administration building, and most recently, a chapel.

A Master Plan Workshop

One secret to his success, Harris says, is to communicate with the church members. "I listen to the people from the church. I'm not going to go in there and tell them 'this is what you want.'"

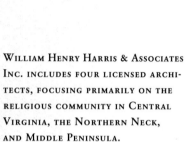

WILLIAM HENRY HARRIS & ASSOCIATES INC. INCLUDES FOUR LICENSED ARCHITECTS, FOCUSING PRIMARILY ON THE RELIGIOUS COMMUNITY IN CENTRAL VIRGINIA, THE NORTHERN NECK, AND MIDDLE PENINSULA.

WILLIAM HENRY "HARRY" HARRIS III IS ONE OF THE BUSIEST AND MOST SUCCESSFUL DESIGNERS OF CHURCH FACILITIES AND BUILDINGS FOR RELIGIOUS ORGANIZATIONS IN THE REGION.

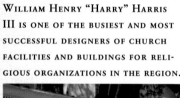

WITH MORE THAN $20 MILLION
OF WORK UNDER CONSTRUCTION,
WILLIAM HENRY HARRIS & ASSOCIATES
INC. PROVIDES CLIENTS WITH SERVICES
THAT INCLUDE MASTER PLANNING,
FEASIBILITY STUDIES, RENOVATION,
HISTORIC PRESERVATION DESIGN, AND
ARCHITECTURAL AND INTERIOR DESIGN.

Over the years, Harris has developed what he calls a "master plan workshop," which is a process that enables him to interact with numerous church members who help him see what they want, both in the short and long term.

"I take all that information and consider it, and I condense it into a plan. It's an approach that has been effective. It enables the entire church community to participate in what's going on, which makes them stakeholders in the project."

Churches are unusual in that they are composed of so many features that are challenging to the architect, Harris says. A fellowship hall is like a restaurant with a commercial kitchen and a large eating area. The education space is equivalent to a high school, with classrooms that can handle different-sized groups as well as modern technology. And many churches include family life centers, which are gymnasiums that can handle sports as well as large group gatherings. The church sanctuary is a great theater that must accommodate a variety of activities. Acoustics, sight lines, lighting, and spaces for a choir and the audience all must be taken into account.

"The modern church is a multimedia experience," Harris says. "It has to be accommodating, because we're catering to generations that have been raised with that expectation." And often he finds himself dealing with historic buildings that require great care, and always, he deals with tender feelings. "People love their church. It is a center of focus for a community. You have to be very sensitive."

A Bright Future

Harris has a specific focus for growing his firm. "We would like to grow a little more, and may open a branch office one day. What we really hope to do is continue to hone our skills as the prime designer of churches in this area.

"Richmond is my home," Harris concludes. "There's a strong religious community here. I love working with all the different people, the different traditions, all the history. I'm pretty satisfied with the work we do. I enjoy working with the people, listening to what their dreams are. They get excited about these things. That's the payoff."

Eagle Construction of Virginia, Inc.

As the population of Richmond ages—along with that of the rest of the United States—housing needs are also changing. Eagle Construction of Virginia, Inc. has been taking steps to keep pace with those changes. Founded in 1984 by Bryan Kornblau, CEO, the firm has established a reputation as one of Richmond's largest builders of single-family residences. Kornblau and Robert W. "Bud" Ohly, president, have worked tirelessly to always stay on the cutting edge of home-building trends.

Eagle has used innovative advertising, designs from nationally recognized architects, and efficient housing construction techniques to create a reputation for providing a lot of home for the money. The firm has grown over the years and was recognized by Integra Realty Resources/Rountrey and Associates, an independent research firm, as the home builder of the decade for the 1990s.

A Complete Developer

Eagle's formula for success has also involved developing its own communities. The firm developed numerous 50- to 100-home communities in Henrico's west end, including Dominion Hills, Linsey Lakes, and Weston. As Kornblau says, "We dis-covered early on that developers were increasing the cost of lots by adding in their profit. We felt we could develop our own communities and pass the savings on to our customers, allow-ing us to provide larger homes and lots for our home buyers at a cost that was less than many of our competitors'. The result was that our homes and communities have been very well received by

◀ DEMENTI-FOSTER STUDIOS

EAGLE CONSTRUCTION OF VIRGINIA, INC. CEO AND FOUNDER BRYAN E. KORNBLAU (LEFT) AND PRESIDENT ROBERT W. OHLY JR. (RIGHT) HAVE SEEN THE COMPANY GROW TO BECOME ONE OF THE LARGEST BUILDERS OF SINGLE-FAMILY RESIDENCES.

EAGLE HAS USED INNOVATIVE ADVERTISING, DESIGNS FROM NATIONALLY RECOGNIZED ARCHITECTS, AND EFFICIENT HOUSING CONSTRUCTION TECHNIQUES TO CREATE A REPUTATION FOR PROVIDING A LOT OF HOME FOR THE MONEY.

consumers who have been pressed to afford the rising cost of housing."

The experience Eagle earned through developing its own smaller communities has led the firm to take that strategy to a higher level. Ohly notes, "We have seen the aging of the population changing the needs of the home buyer to where baby boomers are now desiring a low-maintenance, more active lifestyle than previous generations. Yet these active adults still want to be near their friends and the community amenities they've come to enjoy.

"The result is that we are currently developing the largest active adult community in the Richmond area, with 800 residences in varying styles centered around a community pavilion with indoor swimming and fitness facilities, along with a concierge service. We see that type of community becoming the trend for housing developments as baby boomers continue to age. Single-family residences will always be popular, but demographics dictate that not as many young families will be buying homes and having families, because no generation will be as large as the baby boomers."

Not only are the housing needs of home buyers changing, but they are becoming more demanding as they age. Today's home buyers are more discerning than ever. Eagle has met that challenge through a refinement of its building process to include 18 stages of inspections that will result in a home without a punch list. The punch list has been an institution in home construction since people can remember, but Eagle's process is designed to eliminate it. The company's commitment to customer service will help ensure its continued success as Eagle strives to maintain its position as Richmond's leading home builder.

In addition to instituting an aggressive communication schedule that allows customers to take a more active role in the construction of their homes, Eagle is also developing an Internet-based system for home buyers to access construction, maintenance, and service information about their homes.

Part of the Community

When Eagle is not busy building single-family homes and developing communities to satisfy housing trends, the firm takes on a variety of commercial construction and community service endeavors. The company has constructed more than 1,000 apartment homes, as well as several office/warehouse facilities. Eagle also built the main chapel for the Virginia Home for Boys.

Kornblau and Ohly are both avid golfers and lovers of children, and have worked to make their charitable efforts focus on these two passions. The firm was a principal sponsor of the For Kids' Sake program that built numerous tot lots around Richmond. For years, Eagle sponsored a summer junior golf tour that provided youth in Richmond from all demographic backgrounds the opportunity to play competitive golf at the finest private and public golf courses in the Richmond area for $5 a round. In addition, the firm was integral in bringing a professional golf tournament to Richmond—the Nike Dominion Open, which benefited local charities. The firm has also recently sponsored the WRIC TV8 Rising Stars program to provide school fixtures and equipment for inner-city schools.

Whether it is building a single-family home, developing a community to meet the changing housing needs of an aging population, or working on some charitable endeavor to benefit youth, Eagle Construction of Virginia, Inc. has made a reputation as a firm committed to serving the needs of the people of Richmond.

Richmond Marriott

THE REGION'S LARGEST MEETING AND CONVENTION FACILITY, the Richmond Marriott today stands amid the sights and sounds of a dramatic reawakening throughout the city's old urban hub. The Marriott is renovating and adding services and amenities to meet rising demand in the bustling city center. Since it opened in 1984, the 400-room hotel has maintained a reputation for the high level of

hospitality and efficiency customers have come to expect from Marriott, one of the most respected names in the hotel industry. Hardly a day goes by when the hotel is not playing host to wedding parties, business and government meetings, leisure travelers, sports fans, and the largest conventions that come to central Virginia.

The Richmond Marriott's convenient location, minutes from Interstates 95 and 64, Richmond International Airport, and the Amtrak station, makes it ideal for travelers. The hotel also stands near many major Richmond institutions. From some guest rooms, visitors can see points of interest and activity, including City Hall, the historic Virginia capitol designed by Thomas Jefferson, Virginia Commonwealth University and its Medical College of Virginia Hospitals, and the gleaming Virginia Biotechnology Research Park. It is just an hour's drive to Colonial Williamsburg to the east, and to Charlottesville and the University of Virginia to the west.

Richmond's Gathering Place

With more than 30,000 square feet of flexible space under its roof, and the Richmond Centre for Conventions and Exhibitions a short walk away, the Marriott can accommodate any size meeting, show, exhibition, or event. In addition, the Richmond Centre is currently undergoing a massive expansion that will enable it to house even bigger national conventions.

Also adjoining the Marriott are the Richmond Coliseum, a 14,000-seat sports and entertainment venue, and the popular Festival Park, an outdoor space where concerts and other events draw locals and visitors. The nearby Carpenter Center for the Performing Arts—a restored art deco theater—is slated for expansion, and a new theater complex across Broad Street from the hotel is in the planning stages.

Inside the hotel are lavish ballrooms equipped with modern audiovisual and lighting systems. With crystal chandeliers hanging from high ceilings, the ballrooms have no pillars to impede flow, and they can be divided into smaller meeting rooms. Outside their doors, there is a prefunction foyer, an ideal spot for guest registration,

THE RICHMOND MARRIOTT'S CONVENIENT LOCATION, MINUTES FROM INTERSTATES 95 AND 64, RICHMOND INTERNATIONAL AIRPORT, AND THE AMTRAK STATION, MAKES IT IDEAL FOR TRAVELERS.

receptions, intermissions, and cocktails.

The hotel also contains smaller breakout rooms for parties of 10 to 50, designed for privacy and efficiency, and fully staffed by Marriott professionals. The Executive Boardroom and 15 luxurious suites and parlors are designed for private entertaining and VIP accommodations. Marriott's full-service catering department provides a range of menu choices for luncheons or banquets, for a dozen guests or for 1,200.

Southern Hospitality

Marriott offers express check-in service, free newspaper, and cable TV with premium channels in each room, as well as more than 100 in-room pay movies. Guests appreciate the video-express checkout and in-room message service. Each room is being equipped with high-speed dataports to keep pace with the demands of today's travelers.

Two concierge floors feature even higher levels of service. And the Business Center, open seven days a week, is located in the hotel to provide computer, copying, and faxing services. The hotel also provides notary public and guest laundry services, as well as safe-deposit boxes.

Allie's American Grille serves American cuisine, along with a variety of regional specialties. There is also a lounge in the hotel where guests can enjoy fine cigars and champagne. For the fitness-minded, the hotel contains an indoor pool, tanning salon, outdoor sun deck, sauna, game room, and 24-hour health club with men's and women's locker rooms, Universal gym equipment, Lifecycles, free weights, and other equipment.

The hotel's professional staff is available to coordinate meeting plans, arrange simple coffee breaks or lavish dinners, and set up tours, golf, and other entertainment options. The hotel is minutes from national and regional landmarks and attractions, including the White House of the Confederacy, Virginia Museum of Fine Arts, Science Museum of Virginia, historic Shockoe Slip, Carpenter Center for the Performing Arts, Edgar Allan Poe Museum, Valentine Museum, *Annabelle Lee* riverboat, Children's Museum of Richmond, and the new Richmond Canal Walk.

Marriott Rewards

Regular visitors to Marriott's brand hotels also take advantage of the Marriott Rewards program. Through the program, every dollar spent at one of the company's properties moves the program member closer to free overnight stays, cruises, vacation packages, or frequent flyer miles on

THE HOTEL'S PROFESSIONAL STAFF IS AVAILABLE TO COORDINATE MEETING PLANS, ARRANGE SIMPLE COFFEE BREAKS OR LAVISH DINNERS, AND SET UP TOURS, GOLF, AND OTHER ENTERTAINMENT OPTIONS.

several domestic and international airlines.

And because Marriott has made a major commitment to the Richmond market, the staff at the Richmond Marriott can arrange for visitors to stay at any of nine hotels in the area (five more are under construction), offering a range of services, including moderate-priced accommodations, full-service luxury, and extended-stay rooms.

In addition to this business bond, Richmond and Marriott have worked together on behalf of the community ever since the hotel came to downtown. Since then, Marriott has benefited from business in the region, and it has contributed to a variety of interests, such as Children's Miracle Network, Richmond Children's Hospital, Goodwill, and American Red Cross, whose national convention was headquartered at the hotel. This good-citizen approach, along with quality service and facilities, keeps Marriott and Richmond growing together.

The Berkeley Hotel

SITUATED ON A COBBLESTONED STREET AT A CORNER BETWEEN Richmond's downtown financial district and its center for shopping, dining, and nightlife, The Berkeley Hotel offers elegant surroundings and classic service to visitors to the area. With just 55 individually appointed rooms and an ambience that exudes comfort and warmth, The Berkeley has been providing AAA four-diamond service in a setting that

is both historic and modern since its opening.

The Berkeley offers a generous combination of old European grace and charm and modern comfort and convenience, all with a touch of southern hospitality. Located in the historic Shockoe Slip, the building was constructed to meet the strict architectural requirements that define the district's unique beauty. This careful attention to detail links the structure to its surroundings, often leading visitors to believe the hotel is a much older building.

In fact, The Berkeley, which was built on the site of a parking lot among refurbished brick warehouses and commercial spaces, opened in 1988. Its name was chosen as a link to The Berkeley Castle in England; Berkeley Plantation, just outside Richmond; and Sir William Berkeley, who served as Governor of Virginia during colonial times. Malcolm Jamison, owner of Berkeley Plantation, was the hotel's first guest.

Business Services, Beautiful Places

Although the six-story hotel, with its rich carpets and wood paneling, looks like it has been part of the cityscape for years, The Berkeley's large rooms—with well-appointed bathrooms, plush sitting spaces, and elegant

public spaces—are a suggestion of its modern design. Windows look out onto cobblestoned streets, stylishly restored tobacco warehouses, and Richmond's dramatic downtown skyline. The luxurious Governor's Suite boasts a 30-foot-high vaulted ceiling and terraces overlooking the Shockoe Slip.

The Berkeley's guests enjoy health club privileges, in-room dining, same-day laundry and dry cleaning service, and a classic restaurant. In-room voice mail and Internet connections, a downtown shuttle, and valet parking are available. The hotel's many frequent business travelers also take advantage of secretarial services. Banquet and conference rooms also are available to meet clients' needs, and meeting

and catering staff are available to organize any gathering.

The Berkeley is within easy walking distance of attractions such as Virginia's state capitol, the Canal Walk along the James River, galleries and shops, and a wide range of restaurants and nightspots in Shockoe Slip and Shockoe Bottom. Just up the street at St. John's Church on Church Hill, tourists can visit the spot where Patrick Henry gave his famous "Give me liberty or give me death" speech.

Working for Guests and for the Community

"The secret to The Berkeley's award-winning service is the people," says Director of Sales and Catering Jody

THE BERKELEY HOTEL OFFERS A GENEROUS COMBINATION OF OLD EUROPEAN GRACE AND CHARM AND MODERN COMFORT AND CONVENIENCE, ALL WITH A TOUCH OF SOUTHERN HOSPITALITY.

L. Moore. For its 55 rooms, the hotel has a staff of 75, and many of them have been at The Berkeley for much of the hotel's life.

"That's an excellent ratio, but more important, these are people who understand what this hotel is trying to offer, and they are proud to be working to meet our goals," says Moore, who has worked in the hospitality industry since 1981. Her experience covers virtually all aspects of hotel business, including banquet manager, convention director, bridal fair participant, and staff trainer. Moore also represents The Berkeley in such organizations as the Retail Merchants Association of Greater Richmond and the Richmond Chamber of Commerce, which enables her to network for the hotel and its clients.

Moore also is the hotel's leader in its active community service role. She has been involved with the hotel's backing of a wide range of charities such as Meals on Wheels, United Way, Project Exile, Muscular Dystrophy Association, and Hospital Hospitality House. And Berkeley gift certificates are among the most coveted door prizes offered at numerous fund-raisers and other worthwhile events around Richmond.

Executive Chef Brad Haley is also busy around town, working charitable events on the hotel's behalf. Under Haley's direction, The Berkeley's res-

taurant has been awarded the prestigious AAA four-diamond award every year of his tenure; it is the only restaurant in Richmond to have earned such a rating. The restaurant also was named Virginia's Wine Restaurant of the Year in 1997.

The Berkeley's staff has been coordinated by General Manager Kevin S. Worthy since 1996. Worthy began his career in the hospitality industry in 1979, and his experience has taken him to properties from Orlando to Bermuda. Worthy worked for big-name hospitality leaders, including Sheraton, Holiday Inn, Marriott, and Radisson, before joining The Berkeley.

Worthy represents The Berkeley with the Virginia Hospitality and Travel Association, Virginia Chamber of Commerce, and Retail Merchants

Association of Greater Richmond, among others. He also oversees the hotel's involvement in community affairs such as the Charter House and the Maymont Foundation.

With more than 150,000 guests and visitors having passed through it since the hotel opened in 1988, The Berkeley has come to be recognized as a Richmond institution as a result of its historic location, superior facilities and service, and ongoing contributions to good causes in the community. "This is a place that provides wonderful accommodations, individual service, and a restaurant as good as you'll find in town," says Moore. "Put that all together, and we accomplish our goal, which is to make every guest as comfortable as possible."

ALTHOUGH THE SIX-STORY HOTEL, WITH ITS RICH CARPETING AND WOOD PANELING, LOOKS LIKE IT HAS BEEN PART OF THE CITYSCAPE FOR YEARS, THE BERKELEY'S LARGE ROOMS—WITH WELL-APPOINTED BATHROOMS, PLUSH SITTING SPACES, AND ELEGANT PUBLIC SPACES—ARE A SUGGESTION OF ITS MODERN DESIGN.

Holiday Inn Select-Koger South Conference Center

In 1988, METROPOLITAN RICHMOND'S SOUTHWESTERN CORNER in Chesterfield County seemed like a long way from almost anywhere. That was the year Vernon E. LaPrade and his partners, with an eye to the future, took over the management of a two-year-old Holiday Inn there. Today, the Holiday Inn Select-Koger South Conference Center is Richmond's largest suburban conference center, with 25,000 square feet of

meeting space, 700 free parking spaces, and facilities to accommodate more than 1,000 people for events such as regional association meetings, conferences, trade fairs, weddings, business meetings, reunions, and sporting events.

And just as LaPrade envisioned, no longer is the hotel a long way from anywhere. Today, it is in the middle of one of Chesterfield County's busiest commercial corners at Midlothian Turnpike and Koger Center Boulevard.

The Place to Be

At Holiday Inn Select, guests can walk across the street to Chesterfield Towne Center, one of the largest, most modern shopping centers in the area. Looking out the hotel's windows, they can watch tennis players—sometimes the pros—on the courts at Robious Sports and Fitness Club. For a daily fee, guests have access to the indoor and outdoor courts, indoor Olympic pool, water park, and fitness facilities at Robious. In addition, golf packages to several of the area's top courses are available.

Just beyond Robious is Chesterfield County's Huguenot Park, which offers open spaces, picnic shelters, and respite from urban stress. And nearby, there are dozens of additional shops,

restaurants, and attractions from ice skating and roller skating to movies, laser games, and bowling.

Business Matters

For many of the hotel's guests, business comes first, and the hotel's designation as a Holiday Inn Select indicates that the facility offers enhanced in-room and on-site amenities. Here, each guest room is equipped with two phones, high-speed Internet access, voice mail, data ports, coffeemakers, microwave ovens, refrigerators, irons and ironing boards, and hair dryers, as well as well-lit work areas. Washers and dryers are available, as is a hotel laundry service. The hotel also has on staff a team of certified meeting planners, event coordinators, and other professionals to provide business services.

Recent, $5 million renovations to the hotel have enhanced its meeting facilities. The building can now accommodate dinners for 500 and 700 simultaneously, and it offers a dedicated hospitality suite adjoining the conference center. In addition, there are smaller breakout session rooms near the large ballrooms, and a business center with fax, copier, and data workstations is nearby.

The hotel also contains a cocktail and coffee bar the popular nightclub Visions; an enclosed, heated pool;

and a full-service restaurant. It is convenient to the Powhite Parkway as well, which means it is only a few minutes from downtown Richmond, Richmond International Airport, and Interstates 64 and 95.

Fit for the Stars

In 1998, a new wing of the hotel was built with several rooms clustered around minisuites. This arrangement has proven to be functional and popular for business teams, family groups, and wedding parties that want space together.

The hotel, the tallest building in Chesterfield County, offers two top-floor presidential suites—one containing a large whirlpool bath—and both are equipped with conference facilities and wet bars. The suites have provided overnight lodging for former Wimbledon champion Jimmy Connors, country music star Garth Brooks, and even the Olympic flame.

Recently, the Holiday Inn Select received Holiday Hospitality's Torchbearer Award, designating the hotel as one of 78 Holiday Inn franchises worldwide that continuously exceed the highest standards of excellence. Winning this award represents recognition of the top levels of service and convenience the Holiday Inn Select offers to all its guests.

ℱROM ITS BEGINNING AT A SINGLE LOCATION IN RICHMOND'S West End, Mexico Restaurant has grown into one of the region's success stories. This family business has built on its reputation for providing fine food and friendly service in a festive atmosphere. Today, the Mexico Restaurant operates six unique neighborhood eateries throughout the Richmond metropolitan area, bringing the wealth and breadth of Mexico's cuisine to thousands of loyal diners.

Since 1990, when the Garcia family from Guadalajara opened its first Richmond restaurant on Horsepen Road, the business has grown to employ about 60 people in dining rooms richly decorated with beautiful murals featuring scenes from all over Mexico.

Jose and Raul Garcia—with uncle Jesus Arellano and his son Agustin—started the restaurant. Soon, their sister Maria Garcia and their parents added their energy and expertise to the family business. Over the years, the restaurants have expanded gradually. "Our philosophy has been to bring people into the business as we've needed them and to reward those who contribute most with part ownership in the business," Maria Garcia says. "They share in the business as it grows. It helps them and it helps us, too. It becomes this great, extended family."

Festive Fare
Maria Garcia says these restaurants are distinguished from many others that serve Mexican food by their top-quality, healthy foods and by the distinctive dining spaces. "People today are more health conscious, and we know that," she says. At Mexico, customers have come to expect the freshest ingredients in dishes ranging from the typical tacos and burritos to those that feature sophisticated sauces and unusual tastes. It's not surprising, then, that Mexico's menu is described as "a fiesta for your mouth."

Having come into Richmond at the beginning of a period of dramatic growth in both the size and diversity of the population, Mexico has expanded steadily, adding locations in different parts of town, capturing a loyal customer base.

"The Richmond community has grown so much in the past 10 years," Maria Garcia says. "We were in the right place at the right time." Today, the restaurants attract a variety of people, though they are particularly popular with families. "We've seen children grow up right in front of us," she adds. "The whole community has responded really well to all that we've worked so hard to offer."

Part of the Community
Being involved with the community also has been important to the restaurants' owners and staff. They sponsor a variety of charitable events, such as fund-raising drives for the March of Dimes and children's charities, Maria Garcia says. The restaurants also help out when school groups, teams, and organizations come calling. "We are very active, very local," she explains.

Mexico Restaurant's extended family will probably expand further in years to come. "That's important to the business overall, and it's important to our employees, who recognize that expansion means additional opportunities for them. They know that if they work hard, they may be part owner of the next restaurant," Maria Garcia says. "This is a true family business. We want even the customers to feel that way about it. That way, they will keep coming back."

MEXICO RESTAURANT OPERATES SIX UNIQUE NEIGHBORHOOD EATERIES THROUGHOUT THE RICHMOND METROPOLITAN AREA, BRINGING THE WEALTH AND BREADTH OF MEXICO'S CUISINE TO THOUSANDS OF LOYAL DINERS.

AN INNOVATION IN OFFICE DESIGN, MODULAR OFFICE SYSTEMS have quickly replaced the old office setup of fixed spaces with wooden furniture, the norm for decades. Modular systems, which offer numerous advantages, are less expensive and more flexible for the changing needs of the more modern clients. Over time, corporations became unable to manage existing, excess, or aging office inventories. Richmond-based

Open Plan Systems, founded in 1989, responded to these issues by offering an alternative, and is now one of the nation's largest remanufacturers of name-brand office systems.

"We came into the business at a time when the first major quantities of surplus used product were coming into the marketplace," says Steve Hindle, vice president of sales and marketing. "The clients' initial inclination was to throw out their old products and purchase new systems. Our idea was to reuse the material that could be revitalized instead of throwing it away. We give it a new life at an attractive price."

A National Player

At the outset of the 21st century, Open Plan Systems has moved beyond its image as a local remanufacturer and has emerged as a significant national player in the market for office furniture. Today, Open Plan Systems has 10 sales offices, as well as a remanufacturing plant in Richmond, Virginia,

employing some 160 people. Clients include Texas Instruments, State of North Carolina, Volvo, Lockheed-

Martin, U.S. Department of Defense, General Dynamics, Scott & Stringfellow, Medical College of Virginia, and University of Virginia. Open Plan Systems remains the only remanufacturer to be listed on contract with the U.S. General Services Administration.

Since 1996, the company has been publicly traded, with corporate sales growing each year. Revenues in 2000 exceeded $40 million.

Open Plan Systems remanufactures brand-name office workstations from Herman Miller™. Components are disassembled and metal pieces are cleaned, painted, and oven cured. "We reuse materials without detracting from the products' functionality and, in the end, enhance the outward appearance," Hindle says.

In little more than 10 years, Open Plan Systems has spared more than 50 million tons of workstations from being disposed of in U.S. landfills. Frequently, Open Plan Systems will take a business' old systems as a trade-in against a remanufactured systems purchase with the firm's Asset Banking program.

OPEN PLAN SYSTEMS IS TODAY ONE OF THE NATION'S LARGEST REMANUFACTURERS OF NAME-BRAND OFFICE SYSTEMS AND IS A SIGNIFICANT NATIONAL PLAYER IN THE OFFICE EQUIPMENT MARKET.

efficiently, and that equals a low cost for the customer."

In addition to providing jobs and an environmental alternative for workstations in the community, Open Plan Systems' employees and administration are actively involved in various local charitable concerns. They contribute toys and help sponsor events at the Richmond Children's Hospital, raise funds for the Diabetes Walk-A-Thon, and donate furniture to Noah's Children, Virginia's hospice for children. The company also participates in the Angel Tree drive, which helps less fortunate children during the holiday season; adopts a family through United Way; and participates as a sponsor of the March of Dimes golf tournament.

At Home in Richmond

For Open Plan Systems, Richmond continues to be a good home. "We have been successful hiring here," says Hindle. "We have a diverse workforce that's made up of good people. This is an attractive place to live, and our company is an attractive place to work. Our intention is to continue growing here by improving our performance to meet the demands of customers and continuing our sustainability pledge to the environment."

OPEN PLAN SYSTEMS REMANUFACTURES BRAND-NAME OFFICE WORKSTATIONS FROM HERMAN MILLER™. COMPONENTS ARE DISASSEMBLED AND METAL PIECES ARE CLEANED, PAINTED, AND OVEN CURED.

"We pride ourselves on being able to offer good-as-new quality from both cosmetic and functional points of view, while saving the customer money and giving them delivery and service," Hindle says. "And we are proud to make an environmental contribution, which has a strong appeal to many of our customers. At Open Plan Systems, we are pursuing sustainability while providing a top-quality product."

While remanufacturing makes sense from a cost standpoint, it also makes good environmental sense. By eliminating waste, value is created for customers, who see this value in the form of both the lower initial price and the trade-in value of office workstation assets. Open Plan Systems' Asset Banking program provides a smart option when the time comes to update office space; customers are given a credit for their old systems against an Open Plan Systems' remanufactured systems purchase. This option is good for customers, good for business, and good for the environment. Sustainability just makes sense.

Open Plan Systems' headquarters also functions as a showroom for its products. Hindle states, "We can bring customers in and show them exactly what we do and how we do it. It's an ideal situation." And the firm's location in an industrial center of the city also works well. "In terms of economics, this gives us a big advantage," says Hindle. "A lot of this business is logistics. We can get things to where they need to be quickly and

IN LITTLE MORE THAN 10 YEARS, OPEN PLAN SYSTEMS HAS SPARED MORE THAN 50 MILLION TONS OF WORKSTATIONS FROM BEING DISPOSED OF IN U.S. LANDFILLS.

Hᴀʟɪꜰᴀx Cᴏʀᴘᴏʀᴀᴛɪᴏɴ ɪꜱ ᴀ ʟᴇᴀᴅɪɴɢ ᴘʀᴏᴠɪᴅᴇʀ ᴏꜰ ɪɴꜰᴏʀᴍᴀtion technology (IT), computer maintenance, and communications services nationwide. Its network of professionals supports and manages more than 250,000 pieces of equipment in more than 20,000 locations throughout the country. ⬡ As a technology leader, Halifax has always anticipated industry trends and client needs well in advance. The company has

been creating Web sites and Internet applications since 1995. Also, Halifax performed one of the first Windows 2000 implementations in the world, and received an award from Microsoft for this effort.

Halifax has been providing technology solutions in Richmond for more than 10 years. In that time, the company has developed several mutually beneficial relationships with Richmond-area businesses and government agencies. Current clients include the Virginia Department of Transportation, Virginia Retirement System, Medical College of Virginia Hospitals Authority, and Bon Secours. In addition, Halifax is contracted to provide seat management services to the Commonwealth of Virginia.

"Richmond is an extremely important market for Halifax Corporation," says Douglas E. Mulvihill, marketing manager. As state and local govern-

ments, as well as businesses in and around Richmond, embrace technology and establish partnerships with technology companies, Halifax can bring new products and technical expertise to the region.

Comprehensive Technology Solutions

Based in Alexandria, Virginia, Halifax was founded in 1967. The company has been in Richmond since 1990, and today employs about 100 people in the area, working—as the company has for more than 30 years—to empower enterprises with technology solutions. With more than 50 locations from coast to coast, Halifax employs experienced professionals whose skills and capabilities can create innovative solutions. Traded on the American Stock Exchange, Halifax is a publicly owned company with a commitment to providing superior service through collabo-

ration with customers to meet their specific needs.

Halifax's strength is an ideal combination of experience, skilled employees, and key vendor partnerships that position the company to provide comprehensive technology solutions. The firm has earned authorizations from industry leaders such as Microsoft, Compaq, Cisco, CheckPoint, IBM, Dell, and Surf Control. Halifax provides a wide variety of IT services to the Richmond marketplace. Primary practices include computer maintenance services, information security, professional services, and seat management.

Technology Services That Solve Problems

In the rapidly changing technology environment, Halifax offers an array of services to help almost any business. The company's seat management model

has proved to be a successful way for businesses to acquire and manage their IT investments by resolving common problems of IT departments. This comprehensive plan transfers PC desktop responsibility from the enterprise to a private contractor who manages desktops, printers, and servers through their complete life cycle, significantly reducing total costs and internal IT requirements. In addition, desktop users benefit from regularly scheduled technology refreshment, which ensures that their productivity is enhanced by the most current technology.

Halifax is also a leader in providing information security. The company's comprehensive product and service capabilities allow for centralization of an enterprise's security program, which results in reduced costs and more consistent security policies. From assessments to implementation and ongoing monitoring, Halifax can provide effective fire walls, antivirus products, intrusion detection, E-mail scanning, Web filtering, encryption, alerting strategies, vulnerability testing, and more. The Halifax approach includes not just security products, but also a consultative partnership to help organizations develop security policies to protect from threats that harm network and employee productivity.

Halifax's Professional Services group is responsible for delivering quality-based outsourcing, consulting, staff augmentation, and placement services to clients. The emphasis is on furnishing effective IT personnel and project solutions, as opposed to simply providing bodies or skill sets. The group's objective is to provide flexible and reliable alternatives for delivery of quality consulting services to clients, and to promote consultant growth in a business environment that offers a defined career path and skill development opportunities. Halifax's goal is to become a vital component of an organization's IT environment.

As a computer maintenance provider since 1967, Halifax provides maintenance services on a nationwide basis. The company furnishes on-site maintenance and warranty support for all major manufacturers and for systems such as PCs, servers, printers, midrange systems, software, retail systems, and communications equipment. The firm's staff engineers, each with an average of more than 18 years of experience, are dispatched around the clock from Halifax's National Customer Support Center. The company's depot services capability allows its staff engineers to provide

advanced exchange repair and return, spares support, and staging services through two state-of-the-art facilities.

Halifax's Network Infrastructure group has the ideal combination of experienced, certified engineers; proven project managers; and key industry partners to perform a wide range of integration projects, as well as to perform in-demand service programs. The group offers a mix of national coverage, multivendor and multisystem support, customized service programs, and project management expertise. Services include network architecture and design, messaging and collaboration, desktop management, and network support. The result is a single source for all network service needs.

Halifax Corporation has played a part in Richmond's emergence as a technology market, according to Mulvihill. "Being situated near the high-technology and Internet hub of northern Virginia, and with a highly skilled and affordable technical workforce, many companies, including Halifax, have benefited from tremendous growth in this region," he says. Both the company and the community anticipate that the benefits will continue well into the future.

HALIFAX HAS BEEN PROVIDING TECHNOLOGY SOLUTIONS IN RICHMOND FOR MORE THAN 10 YEARS. IN THAT TIME, THE COMPANY HAS DEVELOPED SEVERAL MUTUALLY BENEFICIAL RELATIONSHIPS WITH RICHMOND-AREA BUSINESSES AND GOVERNMENT AGENCIES.

Founded in Richmond in 1992, Community Pride offers proof that surviving in the grocery business is about more than simply having goods on the shelves and shopping carts. Instead, says Jonathan F. "Johnny" Johnson, president and CEO, the grocery business is a matter of finding out what people in a given community need and then bringing it to them. ❧ "Community Pride is a full-service retail grocery chain that offers minority businesses and customers excellent service, quality products, and clean facilities," Johnson explains. "We do this every day so that other inner-city businesses will see our success and follow our example. Our forte is incorporating our business philosophy into revitalizing underperforming locations throughout the city."

Unique Services for Customers

Established as Community Pride Food Stores, the company began as a chain of four retail grocery stores. Since then, Johnson's chain has grown to six Community Pride locations. These stores serve more than 100,000 customers a week.

"Our customers represent a broad range of socioeconomic groups in the Richmond metropolitan area, although the majority of the communities we serve are from Richmond's inner-city neighborhoods," Johnson says.

Community Pride controls a 7 percent share of the Richmond-Petersburg market, totaling more than $100 million in sales. The company offers an array of services that is unique among retail grocery chains, and these services have proved popular with its customers, who have grown to be a loyal clientele.

Johnson's stores offer a van service to help customers who would otherwise have to walk home with their groceries. Community Pride also offers senior citizens rides to their doctors' appointments. Johnson believes that serving customers means going the extra mile, which is why he used his van service to ferry inner-city residents to the voting polls on Election Day, purely as a community service.

Award-Winning Commitment to People

Johnson's commitment to his business and community has earned him several awards, including the Board of Inner City Partnership Award; the 1999 Strong Men and Women Excellence in Leadership Award from Virginia Power; the 1999 Social Compact Award; and the 2000 Top 40 (executives) Under 40 honor from *Inside Business*, a Richmond business journal.

This mission of service to the community at large is reflective of Community Pride's commitment to the people within the company's ranks as well. "Our pledge to help the customers who support our success would ring hollow if we did not seek to help our own employees survive and thrive," Johnson says.

With this in mind, Community Pride offers its employees programs for continuing studies, work incentives, and management training. "We believe that working for a company should be more than just a paycheck," Johnson says. "It should be a place for personal growth and development."

Jonathan F. "Johnny" Johnson's Community Pride chain of grocery stores has put pride back into Greater Richmond communities. As an award-winning minority entrepreneur, Johnson ensures that his chain of grocery stores works to revitalize underperforming areas throughout the city.

*S*INCE ITS FOUNDING IN 1995, BROOKS BUILDING COMPANY HAS established itself as a high-quality provider of construction services throughout central Virginia. With a variety of repeat clientele and a growing list of notable projects to its credit, Brooks has earned a reputation for delivering small to medium-sized jobs in a timely manner and at a fair cost. ✤ Says Glen K. Brooks, founder and president, "Our goal is for the

customer to have a pleasant experience. That means no surprises during or after the construction. It means proper communication and quality work at a good price."

Finding a Niche in the Market

The Brooks Building Company had its beginning in England. Brooks' father started in the construction industry in London after World War II, and he remains active in the business today. Brooks came to Richmond to attend the University of Richmond on a track scholarship, and he landed a job with a local contractor and developer. After about 10 years, he saw an opportunity to make a difference.

Brooks set out to fill a niche in the market for smaller contractors who could provide professional services somewhere between "the small guy working out of the back of a pickup truck and the major contractors." His intention was to move slowly, starting at about $1 million, putting up commercial buildings. But the market was booming, and Brooks' reputation grew with it. In 2000, the company constructed $7.5 million in projects that ranged from a few hundred dollars to $2.6 million. "Our timing was good, and the community was receptive," Brooks says.

Much of the Brooks Company's work has been medical offices, class-A office space, and retail construction. Its client list includes many of the region's top developers, businesses, and attractions, such as Bank of America, Brandywine Realty Trust, Cendant Incentives, First Union National Bank, Harrison & Bates, HCA/Columbia, Henrico Doctors Hospital, Highwoods Properties, Lewis Ginter Botanical Gardens, McKesson Medical Management, Raycom Media, S.L. Nusbaum Realty, Verizon Wireless, Virginia Cardiovascular Specialists, and Wachovia Bank.

"And many of these are repeat clients," Brooks says, "which is a huge personal mission of mine. We have built a list of repeat clients, and you only see that when you do the job to their satisfaction."

Providing Careful Planning

The secret to such success is providing careful planning, skilled managers on each job, and a careful eye to the bottom line. And it means working with the best subcontractors available. "If you can't use the best, you won't be the best," says Brooks. Trust, not size, is the key to success, and at Brooks Company, customers see that firsthand.

Brooks also takes pride in his company's ability to "fast track" projects, which is one advantage of being a smaller company. Brooks can make decisions on the spot. Clients can come into his office at any time to check on progress. "Through our frequent and informative interaction, we are able to develop relationships based on trust," Brooks says.

Brooks' success is apparent. In 2000, the company saw 20 percent growth. With 10 employees, Brooks says he has no intention of becoming a bigger contractor. "We want to keep up with demand," he says, "and we want to be recognized as the right company for jobs where the client wants personal service and high-quality work. We take a straightforward approach, and that keeps customers coming back to work with us again."

SINCE ITS FOUNDING IN 1995, BROOKS BUILDING COMPANY HAS ESTABLISHED ITSELF AS A HIGH-QUALITY PROVIDER OF CONSTRUCTION SERVICES THROUGHOUT CENTRAL VIRGINIA.

In its relatively short time in Richmond, Infineon Technologies has established itself as a valuable presence in the community, as well as a top competitor among the world's largest semiconductor manufacturers. Established in 1996, Infineon Technologies Richmond began manufacturing DRAM (Dynamic Random Access Memory) products in August 1998, less than 18 months after construction began on the 800,000-square-foot facility.

Infineon Technologies Richmond is the only U.S. manufacturing site under its Munich-based parent company, Infineon AG, which operates 16 manufacturing sites worldwide. The company prides itself on creating innovative products, leading-edge solutions, and services for the benefit of customers and shareholders. "We pride ourselves in being able to find a better way to do things," says Henry Becker, managing director of Infineon's Richmond facility.

Employing the Region's Most Sophisticated Workforce

The ability to quickly produce, test, and deliver a high-caliber product allows Infineon Technologies Richmond to serve an exclusive list of clients that includes Dell Computers, Sun Microsystems, IBM, Compaq, and Hewlett-Packard. Infineon's high-profile list of clients alone is a testament to the company's ability to stand out among its competitors.

"What's different is our people," says Don Owen, manager of human resources for Infineon Technologies Richmond. By adhering to its far-reaching corporate and cultural visions, Infineon seeks to maximize the element that company officials say is its greatest asset—its workers. Because Infineon makes some of the most advanced microelectronic products in its industry, the company employs a stringent recruitment and screening process to make sure it hires some of its industry's most qualified workers. The goal is to find workers who embody the company's motto, We Never Stop Thinking.

The some 1,800 workers at the Henrico County site share a number of positive traits that allow the company to flourish. Employees throughout the plant must be able to work as a team, as well as to gather and assimilate information quickly and efficiently. And because the manufacture of semiconductors takes place under tightly controlled environmental conditions, the plant's workers must be able to keenly observe the most minor details. Maintaining the integrity of the manufacturing facility's dust-free clean room is vital to the production of leading-edge DRAMs.

Becker says Infineon's workers are constantly encouraged to think outside the box and challenge assumptions to streamline the plant's operations. That means that the plant's managers and workers set aggressive production goals, which require a greater output from year to year, while cutting costs at the same time. "We have to reduce our costs about 30 percent per year to remain competitive," Becker says. To do this, Becker says, Infineon's managers ask the workers to challenge assumptions and find the most efficient business and production practices.

And to drive the company's growth, managers and workers alike set aggressive goals for production, continually raising the bar on what Infineon can do. "We don't always know how we're going to get there, but we challenge ourselves to find new ways to get there," Becker says.

It is this attitude that enabled Infineon to earn the distinction of 1999 Fab of the Year, an honor be-

ESTABLISHED IN 1996, INFINEON TECHNOLOGIES RICHMOND IS ONE OF THE WORLD'S LARGEST MANUFACTURERS OF DYNAMIC RANDOM ACCESS MEMORY (DRAM) CHIPS.

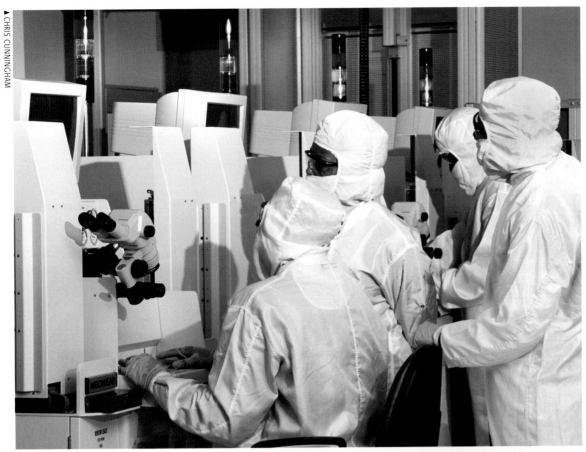

MAINTAINING THE INTEGRITY OF THE MANUFACTURING FACILITY'S DUST-FREE CLEAN ROOM IS VITAL TO THE PRODUCTION OF TOP-FLIGHT DRAMs.

stowed on the company by *Semiconductor International* magazine. To win the magazine's award, Infineon had to meet a long list of stringent criteria that compared the company across the board to all of its competitors. The award recognizes Infineon's performance not only as a manufacturer, but also as an employer and as a member of its local community.

Education Is the Key

Among Infineon's many goals for the Richmond community is ensuring that the area can continue to grow as a technology center. Through a number of partnerships with local government and educational institutions, Infineon seeks to give both its employees and students of all ages access to the technology applications in its industry.

In Henrico County, Infineon Technologies helped establish the High Tech Academy—an educational program for highly motivated students—which prepares students for post-secondary training at two- or four-year institutions in the field of engineering or other technology-related curricula. Students also learn the academic and technical skills required to be successful in obtaining employment immediately upon graduating from the High Tech Academy.

"They're really getting an academic education through application," says

Becker. To perform their laboratory experiments, the students must wear "bunny suits" that protect the lab's clean room from human hair and dust particles. "We do a lot of educational investment, not only in the local community, but also for our employees," Becker says.

Infineon's employees benefit from educational partnerships with Virginia Commonwealth University, J. Sargent Reynolds Community College, and John Tyler Community College. Through these alliances, Infineon's employees have access to college courses at a variety of locations, including the facility where they work. This easy access helps workers meet

demanding work schedules and continue their education while having time for family and outside interests.

Richmond Embraces Technology

Becker and Owen both say that the good quality of life Richmond offers is one of the key factors that drew Infineon to Richmond. And they point to the business incentives that Virginia and the local municipalities have offered Infineon Technologies Richmond as examples of how the manufacturer has been welcomed into the area. "All of these things and the nature of the workforce have left us very pleased with our experience in the Richmond area," Becker says.

STUDENTS ACCEPTED TO THE HIGH TECH ACADEMY EARN COLLEGE CREDITS WHILE OBTAINING THEIR HIGH SCHOOL DIPLOMAS.

ℙROVIDING FREEDOM FOR PATIENTS, EMPLOYEES, AND REFERRAL sources is the driving force behind the business plan of Freedom, Inc. Home Health. Established in Richmond in January 1997 by Deborah A. Hackman, R.N., B.S.N., Freedom admits close to 15 patients per day, serves approximately 4,000 patients, makes more than 45,000 visits per year, and has more than 200 employees and 1,000 referral sources.

Medicare certified and accredited by the Joint Commission on Accreditation of Healthcare Organizations, Freedom provides home health services for those who qualify for Medicare Part A Home Health Services, as well as for those adults and/or children with insurance coverage that contracts Freedom to be a provider. Freedom's goal is not to grow or expand, but instead to focus intentionally on a strategy, which includes staying centered on the company's mission "to provide quality care and quality service with quality professionals."

The staff and management at Freedom believe that staying focused on the company's mission and strategy will lead to success, and that focusing on growing for the purpose of becoming bigger or making more money is inappropriate and a strategy for failure. They also believe that success is not quantified in the number of visits, admissions, or episodes, but in the satisfaction of patients, referral sources, and employees.

Attracting and Retaining the Best Employees

To attract and retain the best employees, Freedom demonstrates its belief that people are its most important asset. Creating an atmosphere that employees love takes time, effort, and money, with the reward coming when recruitment is easy, attrition is low, and morale is high. To positively affect the lives of each employee, Freedom sponsors an annual Freedom Night at the Baseball Diamond; an annual bus trip to Colonial Williamsburg; an annual Freedom Picnic at Liberty Farm; and an annual dinner banquet where achievement awards are presented. The company's president sends birthday cards to all employees, and notes or cards of encouragement are given to employees who go above and beyond the call of duty.

Quality care and excellent service alone do not differentiate one company from others. Freedom believes that while personal aspiration to provide quality care and service is the purpose for going into the home health business, it is not possible to succeed without quality professionals.

Prospective Payment System

When the Prospective Payment System (PPS) began in October 2000, the system brought with it many challenges. It was then, and continues now to be, imperative to have a team empowered to make informed decisions swiftly. Freedom's senior management became capable of responding to the potential adversity of PPS by providing the team with the education necessary to make the program work. With its knowledge of PPS, Freedom is in a position to take those high-cost patients that other agencies turn away.

The Freedom team used several actions to overcome the potential adversity to PPS. Among these actions were the development of clinical pathways and educational tools that enabled clinicians to be more effective and efficient in the field, as well as the development of a comprehensive plan for educating the administrative staff. Freedom also conducted quarterly meetings for performance improvement, budget, and ethics; held monthly meetings for leadership and

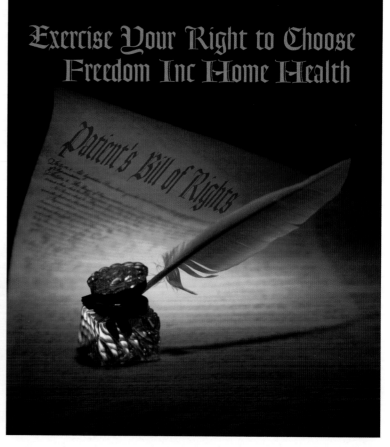

senior management to evaluate appropriateness, adequacy, effectiveness, efficiency, long-term growth, and operational improvement; and conducted weekly clinical management and administrative meetings.

Value-Added Services

Freedom is in the process of becoming an industry leader with the implementation of a strategic clinical plan that differentiates it from other home health agencies. The development of disease-specific programs adds value to home health care. Some of the specific components Freedom uses in its cardiac program are an education program whereby nurses can become competent, proficient, or expert cardiac nurses; clinical pathways for each cardiac disease process that leave no stone unturned for assessment, physician's routine orders, nursing action plans, and teaching materials; and the purchase of cardiac equipment that is easy to use and sends the data over the phone from the patient's home to the computer in Freedom's office.

Freedom's cardiac program, and others like it, adds value to the quality of the company's patient care and makes its patients, as well as physicians, happy. In addition, the programs have had a tremendous effect on the clinical and administrative team at Freedom, Inc., such as consistency among clinicians in documentation; the opportunity to measure outcomes and track best practices through questions and answers; a decrease in the denial rate due to documentation errors; the best opportunity for clinicians to be efficient and effective in the home; and a system that lets nurses who do follow-up visits know exactly what patient care has or has not been done, thereby increasing the efficiency and effectiveness of weekend clinicians. Creating value for patients and referral sources, and giving clinicians the tools to do so, is considered the most important thing a home health agency can do for the community.

Freedom, Inc. Home Health stays on top of its game by constantly adapting processes, delivering more value to customers, and dealing with competitive challenges as they emerge. With 99 percent patient and referral satisfaction, Freedom has reached its goals thus far, and will forever strive for continuous quality improvement.

MORE THAN 200 EMPLOYEES—NURSES AND HOME HEALTH AIDES (BOTTOM RIGHT), THERAPISTS (BOTTOM LEFT), AND ADMINISTRATORS (TOP)—GUIDE FREEDOM, INC. HOME HEALTH AS IT WORKS WITH SOME 4,000 PATIENTS ANNUALLY. AT FREEDOM, SUCCESS IS NOT QUANTIFIED IN NUMBER OF VISITS, ADMISSIONS, OR EPISODES, BUT IN THE SATISFACTION OF PATIENTS, REFERRAL SOURCES, AND STAFF MEMBERS.

Networking Technologies and Support, Inc. (NTS) is a full-service systems integrator providing customers with a single source for a broad range of high-technology products and services. Having established a record for high performance, competitive pricing, and financial stability, the company counts some of the largest and most prestigious businesses in the region among its growing list of clients. Because of this,

NTS is positioned to be a key contributor to the region's growth as a center of high-tech business activity.

Solutions to Information Technology Demands

Since its beginnings in Richmond in 1997, NTS has experienced rapid growth. Today, the company employs more than 70 full-time professionals, most of them network or field engineers. NTS' services have evolved into an interrelated set of offerings focused around customized computer hardware maintenance, network integration, enterprise security, product procurement and deployment services, and staff augmentation services.

Bernard E. Robinson, president and CEO, founded NTS after accumulating more than 20 years of corporate marketing and management experience with companies including IBM Corporation, CMS Automation, and Xerox Corporation.

Today, the company's highly skilled technology professionals are capable of providing customized information technology (IT) solutions, managing technology assets, finding staff with the right skill sets, measuring and improving systems performance, and working with and training the end user. NTS was built, and continues to grow, based on the reputation and performance of its employees. As NTS positions itself for the future, the company continues to honor the principles that have been essential to its success.

BERNARD ROBINSON IS PRESIDENT AND CEO OF NETWORKING TECHNOLOGIES AND SUPPORT, INC.

NETWORKING TECHNOLOGIES AND SUPPORT IS DEDICATED TO QUALITY SERVICE AND RAPID RESPONSE.

A Record of Excellence

In 2000, NTS was recognized as one of Ernst & Young's Entrepreneurs of the Year. The award celebrates entrepreneurs who have achieved extraordinary success due to excellence in such areas as innovation, financial performance, and personal commitment to their businesses and communities.

NTS' customer base spans many industries and includes such diverse firms as Bon Secours; Branch Cabell; Troutman, Sanders, Mays & Valentine; Philip Morris; SuperValu/Richfood; SunTrust Bank; Thompson Siegel & Walmsley; and Ukrop's. The company has branched out to serve state, local, and federal government entities, as well as the education market. Customers include the Virginia Lottery, Department of Motor Vehicles, Old Dominion University, Spotsylvania County Government, and Virginia Beach City Public Schools.

NTS is a minority-owned business certified with the Virginia Regional Minority Supplier Diversity Council and the Commonwealth of Virginia's Department of Minority Business Enterprises. The firm is also a member in good standing of the Virginia Chamber of Commerce, Greater

Richmond Chamber of Commerce, Better Business Bureau of Richmond, and Council of Growing Companies.

People, Products, Networks, and Services

NTS provides technically astute, trained, and certified professionals to augment clients' permanent IT organizations, either on a full-time or a part-time basis. NTS can supplement a client's staff with technicians, systems engineers, analysts, programmers, procurement specialists, and project managers who are trained and licensed by today's leading technology manufacturers. In outsourcing relationships, NTS makes available its complete range of business technology resources, and offers training and technology refresher courses.

NTS also provides state-of-the-art procurement and distribution services, which guarantee fast and accurate fulfillment of purchase orders and deliveries. The firm has access to comprehensive inventories of more than 20,000 products from more than 600 manufacturers. Consequently, NTS ensures that its clients can rapidly deploy—and benefit from—new technologies.

NTS has strong relationships with most major computer distributors. The company's strategy of using multiple suppliers allows it to provide clients with outstanding value, greater product availability, rapid delivery, and excellent technical support service.

Now that the network has taken center stage in corporate America, NTS' technical professionals have become key strategic decision makers. Through years of experience in infrastructure design and supporting solutions around Microsoft and Novell products, NTS has assembled a skilled team of professionals with expertise in customizing and integrating network operating system products. Team members are

trained to help companies utilize technology to meet their business goals.

NTS offers a core of network integration services that include every facet of project implementation. As a Microsoft Solutions Provider and a Novell Gold Partner, NTS' status as a state-of-the-art vendor assures its customers that they are dealing with a firm that can provide current problem resolution and strategic planning. One of the company's largest expenditures is in the area of IT training, which prepares NTS employees to handle each customer's concerns and helps them deploy technology strategically.

A Long-Term Focus

NTS seeks to become one of the largest and best regional providers of computer maintenance services. Currently, the company employs more than 45 engineers, all of them manufacturer certified, in its Field Operations Division. The firm's ability to respond to problems quickly with the right people and resources sets NTS apart from its

competitors. Most important, the company can provide this level of service every day of the year.

As NTS has enjoyed rapid growth, the company has maintained a low employee turnover rate of 2 percent by providing solid management and maintaining high employee morale. In this highly competitive industry, the long-term retention of talented engineers translates into tremendous benefits to customers desiring a long-term business relationship with their technology partner.

Networking Technologies and Support, Inc. was built on principles that still guide it today. The company's workers are well trained, and they continue to stay ahead of the rapidly advancing technology curve. The firm's leaders state that their commitment as a company is to provide 100 percent customer service, to deliver as promised, and to continually improve their knowledge in the IT industry. By following through on this commitment, NTS will play a key role in the region far into the industry's future.

THE NTS MANAGEMENT TEAM IS (FROM LEFT) MARK MANN, BERNARD ROBINSON, MARK ROBERTS, AND STEVE ESTEP.

NTS CAN SUPPLEMENT A CLIENT'S STAFF WITH TECHNICIANS, SYSTEMS ENGINEERS, ANALYSTS, PROGRAMMERS, PROCUREMENT SPECIALISTS, AND PROJECT MANAGERS WHO ARE TRAINED AND LICENSED BY TODAY'S LEADING TECHNOLOGY MANUFACTURERS (RIGHT).

NTS' SERVICES HAVE EVOLVED INTO AN INTERRELATED SET OF OFFERINGS FOCUSED AROUND CUSTOMIZED COMPUTER HARDWARE MAINTENANCE, NETWORK INTEGRATION, ENTERPRISE SECURITY, PRODUCT PROCUREMENT AND DEPLOYMENT SERVICES, AND STAFF AUGMENTATION SERVICES.

Wachovia Bank

interstate financial holding company with a major presence in both the city of Richmond and the state of Virginia. With more than $44 billion in deposits, it does business in regional, national, and international markets. But Wachovia's value to the communities it serves may best be seen in the smile of a child being read to by a Wachovia tutor, by the

handshake between a new home-owner and a Habitat for Humanity volunteer, or by the confidence in a future small-business owner who has just completed a Wachovia seminar.

Since 1879, when it first opened in Winston, North Carolina, to serve farmers, craftsmen, and businesses, Wachovia has been committed to building strong communities. The company has been shaped by people dedicated to a standard of excellence and integrity that has become synonymous with the Wachovia name.

Success Woven from Community Fabric

Virginia became a Wachovia home state in 1997, with the merger of Central Fidelity Banks Inc. and Jefferson Bankshares Inc. of Charlottesville, two leading financial institutions. The two

began operating as Wachovia in March 1998. Today, in the 84 Virginia communities Wachovia serves, the corporation and its employees are meeting community financial needs and public interests, and contributing to economic and social progress.

Indeed, the company prides itself on being an active participant in every community it serves. Its success, the bank's workers realize, is woven from the same fabric as the community. Where these communities are strong, the banks will be strong.

With that philosophy in mind, Wachovia is involved in a variety of programs that benefit communities. One of those is the Wachovia Community Development Corporation (WCDC), through which Wachovia and Fannie Mae, the nation's largest source of financing home mortgages,

work to offer innovative solutions for affordable housing projects in Virginia and throughout the Southeastern United States.

"This new relationship combines the resources and complementary strengths of both WCDC and Fannie Mae to create more affordable housing and community development opportunities in targeted areas of the Southeast," says Fred D. Baldwin, president of WCDC.

Community Leadership is Part of the Business

Wachovia's ranks are full of employees who provide volunteer leadership and donate their time, energy, talents, and dollars to numerous community organizations. Executive leadership is a critical ingredient in Wachovia's commitment. Company executives collaborate with a broad range of community groups and lend expertise to fund-raising drives, capital campaigns for non-profit organizations, United Way campaigns, boards, committees, and community task forces. This support comes from a company-wide recognition that community leadership is an integral part of business activities.

And Wachovia practices what it preaches within the corporation. It has been named by *Working Mother* magazine as one of the 100 best places in the United States to work.

With a record of more than 100 years of providing dependable and quality personal, corporate, and institutional financial services, Wachovia serves 3.8 million consumers and 200,000 small business and business banking customers in Florida, Georgia, North Carolina, South Carolina, and Virginia. With a remarkable continuity of leadership and an unswerving commitment to each community, the company will continue to produce long-term profitable growth while adapting to change and maintaining its core of operating in a sound and prudent manner.

TODAY, IN THE 84 VIRGINIA COMMU-NITIES WACHOVIA BANK SERVES, THE CORPORATION AND ITS EMPLOYEES ARE MEETING COMMUNITY FINANCIAL NEEDS AND PUBLIC INTERESTS, AND CONTRIBUTING TO ECONOMIC AND SOCIAL PROGRESS.

*I*N A GROWING, HIGH-END RESIDENTIAL COMMUNITY, SCHAEDLE Worthington and Hyde Developers—one of the Southeast's most respected developers— recently opened The Grove Swift Creek. Among towering trees and close to Swift Creek Reservoir, The Grove Swift Creek offers one-, two-, and three-bedroom apartment homes with luxury appointments, southern-colonial-style architecture, and convenient features.

Just 15 minutes from downtown Richmond, in the midst of western Chesterfield County, The Grove Swift Creek is designed for people who have found that renting fits their lifestyle, says Sarah Everhart, community manager.

"A lot of people are finding they would rather take $30,000 and invest it and get a higher return quicker [than putting it down on a house]," says Everhart. "So we offer them the country-club lifestyle with home-size floor plans that they want and need to rent comfortably for a long time. We'd like to have our residents stay here forever."

The Grove Swift Creek, which began renting in 1999, contains 240 apartment homes. "This is our company's 17th development, and we've learned over time that this is just the right size," Everhart says. The firm's luxury-oriented approach appeals to a clientele willing to spend more to get more. Most of The Grove Swift Creek's residents are business professionals and families.

Superior Service

"We do spoil our residents," Everhart says. There is a free continental breakfast along with the daily newspapers in the business center each morning. The business center itself contains computers with Internet access and other equipment. A free video library stocks the latest movies. Card access to private entry gates ensures privacy, and the same card allows residents to use other amenities, such as the business center and fitness center, at any time. There's even a pool with lap lanes, and tennis courts as well.

"We're providing amenities that should make residents feel like they're staying in a concierge-style hotel, rather than just renting an apartment," Everhart says.

The apartments contain the area's most spacious floor plans. The one-bedroom units are 889 square feet, those with two bedrooms are 1,150 square feet, and the three-bedroom units are 1,435 square feet. Each Grove Swift Creek apartment has nine-foot ceilings, a ceramic-tiled foyer, a computer space, a linen closet, a pantry, walk-in closets in each bedroom, a private patio or balcony, and a detached garage. "These really are home-sized apartments," Everhart says. "It's a place you're not going to want to move out of."

These days, many rental properties are owned by real estate investment trusts—huge businesses with an orientation toward stockholders rather than residents—but not The Grove Swift Creek. Its developers are its owners, and their intention is to generate profits by keeping residents in the apartments for a long time, Everhart says. The construction crews who built the buildings are employed by the development company. "We're building quality buildings because this is a long-term investment," she says.

The location also speaks to the long term. It's in an up-and-coming area that will soon be linked by a bridge across the James River to another residential area where upscale development is booming. "We're out of the hubbub, but close enough to all the things our residents will want, such as great shopping, restaurants, and entertainment," Everhart says. "You can come home to an almost secluded atmosphere that you know is going to stay that way well into the future."

THE GROVE SWIFT CREEK OFFERS ONE-, TWO-, AND THREE-BEDROOM APARTMENT HOMES WITH LUXURY APPOINTMENTS, SOUTHERN-COLONIAL-STYLE ARCHITECTURE, AND CONVENIENT FEATURES.

BEGINNING AS A SMALL PUBLISHER OF LOCAL NEWSPAPERS IN 1935, Towery Publishing, Inc. today has become a global publisher of a diverse range of community-based materials from San Diego to Sydney. Its products—such as the company's award-winning Urban Tapestry Series, business directories, magazines, and Internet sites—continue to build on Towery's distinguished heritage of excellence, making its name synonymous with service, utility, and quality.

Community Publishing at Its Best

Towery Publishing has long been the industry leader in community-based publications. In 1972, current President and CEO J. Robert Towery succeeded his parents in managing the printing and publishing business they had founded four decades earlier. "One of the more impressive traits of my family's publishing business was its dedication to presenting only the highest-quality products available—whatever our market might be," says Towery. "Since taking over the company, I've continued our fight for the high ground in maintaining this tradition."

During the 1970s and 1980s, Towery expanded the scope of the company's published materials to include *Memphis* magazine and other successful regional and national publications, such as *Memphis Shopper's Guide*, *Racquetball* magazine, *Huddle/FastBreak*, *Real Estate News*, and *Satellite Dish* magazine. In 1985, after selling its locally focused assets, the company began the trajectory on which it continues today, creating community-oriented materials that are often produced in conjunction with chambers of commerce and other business organizations.

All of Towery Publishing's efforts, represented on the Internet at www.towery.com, are marked by a careful, innovative design philosophy that has become a hallmark of the company's reputation for quality and service. Boasting a nationwide sales force, proven editorial depth, cutting-edge graphics capabilities, ample marketing resources, and extensive data management expertise, the company has assembled the intellectual and capital resources necessary to produce quality products and services.

Urban Tapestry Series

Towery Publishing launched its popular Urban Tapestry Series in 1990. Each of the nearly 100 oversized, hardbound photojournals details the people, history, culture, environment, and commerce of a featured metropolitan area. These colorful coffee-table books spotlight communities through an introductory essay authored by a noted local individual, an exquisite collection of photographs, and in-depth profiles of select companies and organizations that form each area's business core.

From New York to Vancouver to Los Angeles, national and international authors have graced the pages of the books' introductory essays. The celebrated list of contributors includes two former U.S. presidents—Gerald Ford (Grand Rapids) and Jimmy Carter (Atlanta); boxing great Muhammad Ali (Louisville); two network newscasters—CBS anchor Dan Rather (Austin) and ABC anchor Hugh Downs (Phoenix); NBC sportscaster Bob Costas (St. Louis); record-breaking quarterback Steve Young (San Francisco); best-selling mystery author Robert B. Parker (Boston); American Movie Classics host Nick Clooney (Cincinnati); former Texas first lady Nellie Connally (Houston); and former New York City Mayor Ed Koch (New York).

While the books have been enormously successful, the company continues to improve and redefine the role the series plays in the marketplace. "Currently, the Urban Tapestry Series works beautifully as a tool for enhancing the image of the communities it portrays," says Towery. "As the series continues to mature, we want it to

TOWERY PUBLISHING, INC. PRESIDENT AND CEO J. ROBERT TOWERY (LEFT) TOOK THE REINS OF HIS FAMILY'S BUSINESS IN 1972, MAINTAINING THE COMPANY'S LONG-STANDING CORE COMMITMENT TO QUALITY.

SORTING THROUGH HUNDREDS OF BEAUTIFUL PHOTOGRAPHS IS JUST ONE OF THE ENVIABLE TASKS ASSIGNED TO TOWERY'S TOP-NOTCH TEAM OF DESIGNERS AND ART DIRECTORS, LED BY AWARD-WINNING CREATIVE DIRECTOR BRIAN GROPPE (LEFT). MEMBERS OF TOWERY'S EDITORIAL STAFF CULL THE BEST FROM MATERIALS SUBMITTED BY FEATURE WRITERS AND PROFILE CLIENTS TO PRODUCE THE URBAN TAPESTRY SERIES (RIGHT).

become a reference source that businesses and executives turn to when evaluating the quality of life in cities where they may be considering moving or expanding."

Chambers of Commerce Turn to Towery

In addition to its Urban Tapestry Series, Towery Publishing has become the largest producer of published and Internet materials for North American chambers of commerce. From published membership directories and Internet listings that enhance business-to-business communication, to visitor and relocation guides tailored to reflect the unique qualities of the communities they cover, the company's chamber-oriented materials offer comprehensive information on dozens of topics, including housing, education, leisure activities, health care, and local government.

The company's primary Internet product consists of its introCity™ sites. Much like its published materials, Towery's introCity sites introduce newcomers, visitors, and longtime residents to every facet of a particular community, while simultaneously placing the local chamber of commerce at the forefront of the city's Internet activity. The sites provide newcomer information including calendars, photos, citywide business listings with everything from nightlife to shopping to family fun, and on-line maps pinpointing the exact location of businesses, schools, attractions, and much more.

Sustained Creativity

The driving forces behind Towery Publishing have always been the company's employees and state-of-the-

art industry technology. Many of its employees have worked with the Towery family of companies for more than 20 years. Today's staff of seasoned innovators totals around 120 at the Memphis headquarters, and more than 40 sales, marketing, and editorial staff traveling to and working in an ever growing list of cities.

Supporting the staff's endeavors is state-of-the-art prepress publishing software and equipment. Towery Publishing was the first production environment in the United States to combine desktop publishing with color separations and image scanning to produce finished film suitable for

burning plates for four-color printing. Today, the company relies on its digital prepress services to produce more than 8,000 pages each year, containing more than 30,000 high-quality color images.

Through decades of business and technological change, one aspect of Towery Publishing has remained constant. "The creative energies of our staff drive us toward innovation and invention," Towery says. "Our people make the highest possible demands on themselves, so I know that our future is secure if the ingredients for success remain a focus on service and quality."

WITH *The Open Container*—AN OUTDOOR SCULPTURE BY MEMPHIAN MARK NOWELL—MARKING THE SPOT, TOWERY'S MEMPHIS OFFICE SERVES AS HEADQUARTERS FOR THE COMPANY'S INNOVATIVE COMMUNITY-BASED PUBLICATIONS.

SISSON

Photographers

A Memphis-based, independent agricultural photojournalist, **WILLIAM E. BARKSDALE** contributes to farm magazines, and his photography has been used in marketing communications by many firms providing input to the farm market. His images have appeared in several other Towery publications.

Originally from Lexington, Virginia, **BOB BROWN** has lived and worked in the Richmond area for more than 40 years. He has earned the Virginia News Photographer of the Year award three times, a Miley Award for Excellence in Photojournalism, and various first-place national and regional awards. He photographs for the *Richmond Times-Dispatch* and enjoys politics.

A photojournalist with the *Richmond Times-Dispatch*, **ALEXA WELCH EDLUND** has photographed and written about her travels in Indonesia, Thailand, South Africa, Zimbabwe, Germany, and Scotland. She earned the 1997 Contributing Journalist Award from the National Center for Farmworker Health, and she has also won various Virginia Press Photographer Association and Virginia Press Association awards.

A self-taught photographer, **DON EILER** specializes in advertising, architectural, corporate, and editorial photography. His images have illustrated *Fighting Men of the Civil War, Commanders of the Civil War, Battlefields of the Civil War, Age of the Gunfighter, An Illustrated History of the U.S. Navy,* and *A History of the African American People.*

A Richmond native, **DAVID L. EVERETTE** specializes in landscape, nature, urban, and black-and-white photography. Once a commercial photographer, he now owns A Better Image, a photography agency.

Employed by David R. McGeorge Mercedes-Benz, **JEFF GARDNER** also freelances for the *Richmond Times-Dispatch*. Several of his images have been published in *Today's Photographer* magazine, and he has covered local news events and sports teams. His images have garnered several awards, and his exhibit about Virginia, *The Old Dominion*, was held in New York City in June 2000.

Founded in 1991, **GEOIMAGERY** is a membership association of photographers, writers, travelers, and natural history enthusiasts. Composed of a group of photographers with a common interest in exploring the world photographically and developing publishing outlets for these images, GeoIMAGERY has grown to more than 200 members with diverse styles and broad coverage.

Originally from New York, **TONY GIAMMARINO** is self-employed at Giammarino & Dworkin, a photography and styling agency. He specializes in interior design, landscape, and still-life photography, and his images have appeared in *Bon Appetit, Country Living*, several Barnes & Noble books, and Rockport Publishing releases.

A news photographer for the *Richmond Times-Dispatch*, **MARK GORMUS** has earned numerous Virginia News Photographer Association and Virginia Press Association awards.

BUD LEE studied at the Columbia University School of Fine Arts in New York and the National Academy of Fine Arts. A self-employed photojournalist, he founded the Florida Photographers Workshop and the Iowa Photographers Workshop. His work can be seen in *Esquire, Life, Travel & Leisure, Rolling Stone*, the *Washington Post*, and the *New York Times*, as well as in several Urban Tapestry Series publications.

© DAVID L. EVERETTE

After studying art in his native Ireland, **James Lemass** moved to Cambridge, Massachusetts, in 1987. His specialties include people and travel photography, and his photographs have appeared in several other Towery publications.

A staff photographer for the *Richmond Times-Dispatch*, **P. Kevin Morley** has earned more than 40 awards for photography from the Virginia News Photographers Association and the Virginia Press Association. A photojournalism instructor at the University of Richmond, he has photographed missionaries in Uganda, the aftermath of civil war in Rwanda, and the aftermath of Hurricane Andrew.

A Richmond native, **Elaine Odell** owns Odell Photography and specializes in commercial, editorial, environmental, portrait, food, and industrial photography. Her images have appeared in *Richmond Magazine*, and her clients include Commerce Bank, YMCA of Greater Richmond, and Virginia Municipal League.

Specializing in people and location photography, **Chuck Savage** owns Savage Productions Inc. He has lived and worked in the Richmond area for more than 20 years, and his images have appeared in several books and magazines.

Owner of Jeff S. Saxman Photography, Inc., **Jeff S. Saxman** specializes in product, architectural, and sports photography. A graduate from Rochester Institute of Technology, he has resided in Richmond for more than 10 years.

David Stover owns David Stover Photography and specializes in advertising, editorial, people on location, and stock photography. A Richmond native, he earned his MFA in photography from Virginia Commonwealth University.

Originally from Richmond, **Charles Taylor** has created CD covers for local jazz artists Walter Bell, Ashby Anderson, and Jason Jenkins.

Formerly a business executive, **Nat Taylor** owns NT Photography and specializes in travel, outdoor, and nature photography. Originally from Williamsburg, he has lived and worked in the Richmond area for more than 45 years.

A Richmond native, **Stuart T. Wagner** specializes in photojournalism and is a network engineer at MCI WorldCom. His images have appeared in *Time*, *Newsweek*, the *Richmond Times-Dispatch*, and a variety of newspapers nationwide.

A freelance photographer for Richmond Publishing, **Alfred Wekelo** specializes in editorial, advertisement, landscape, cityscape, and celebrity portrait photography. A member of the Virginia Press Association, he has won the international photo contest with Phototrust, and his images have appeared in *Richmond Magazine* and *Richmond Parents*. His clients include Clear Channel Broadcasting, Randolph-Macon College, the Solution Group, BonSecours Richmond Health System, and other businesses.

Other contributing photographers and organizations include Clement Britt, Dean Hoffmeyer, Chuck Janus, Joe Mahoney, Bruce N. Parker, the *Richmond Times-Dispatch*, and Stuart T. Wagner. For more information about the photographers appearing in *Greater Richmond: Region on the Rise*, please contact Towery Publishing.

© CHUCK SAVAGE

Library of Congress Cataloging-in-Publication Data

Greater Richmond : region on the rise / introduction by Steve Clark ; art direction by
Brian Groppe ; sponsored by the Greater Richmond Chamber of Commerce.

       p. cm. – (Urban tapestry series)

     Includes index.

     ISBN 1-881096-94-7 (alk. paper)

       1. Richmond Region (Va.)–Civilization. 2. Richmond Region (Va.)–Pictorial works.
3. Richmond Region (Va.)–Economic conditions. 4. Business
enterprises–Virginia–Richmond Region. I. Towery Publishing. II Series.

F234.R55 G74 2001

975.5'45–dc21

                                       2001043076

Printed in China

© PERK GORMUS / RICHMOND TIMES-DISPATCH

Towery Publishing, Inc.
The Towery Building
1835 Union Avenue
Memphis, TN 38104
WWW.TOWERY.COM

PUBLISHER: J. Robert Towery EXECUTIVE PUBLISHER: Jenny McDowell MARKETING
DIRECTOR: Carol Culpepper SALES MANAGER: Bill Koons PROJECT DIRECTOR: Dianne
Thompson EXECUTIVE EDITOR: David B. Dawson MANAGING EDITOR: Lynn Conlee
SENIOR EDITORS: Carlisle Hacker, Brian L. Johnston PROJECT EDITOR/CAPTION WRITER:
Danna M. Greenfield EDITOR/PROFILE MANAGER: Jay Adkins EDITORS: Stephen M.
Deusner, Rebecca E. Farabough, Sabrina Richert, Ginny Yeager PROFILE WRITER: Rob
Walker PHOTOGRAPHY EDITOR: Jonathan Postal PHOTOGRAPHIC CONSULTANT: Perk
Gormus PRODUCTION MANAGER: Laurie Beck PROFILE DESIGNERS: Rebekah Barnhardt,
Glen Marshall PHOTOGRAPHY COORDINATOR: Robin Lankford PRODUCTION
ASSISTANT: Robert Parrish DIGITAL COLOR SUPERVISOR: Darin Ipema DIGITAL COLOR
TECHNICIANS: Eric Friedl, Mark Svetz PRINT COORDINATOR: Beverly Timmons

Index of Profiles

© CHUCK SAVAGE

RICHMOND CITY LIMIT